The Authorities

~ Powerful Wisdom from Leaders in the Field ~

ANDREA NGUI

Award Winning Author

Publisher
Authorities Press
Markham, ON
Canada

Printed in the United States and Canada.

FOREWORD

Experts are to be admired for their knowledge, but they often remain unrecognized by the general public because they save their information and insights for paying customers and clients. There are many experts in a given field, but their impact is limited to the handful of people with whom they work.

Unlike experts, authorities share their knowledge and expertise far more broadly, so they make a big impact on the world. Authorities become known and admired as leading experts and, as such, typically do very well economically and professionally. Most authorities are also mature enough to know that part of the joy of monetary success is the accompanying moral and spiritual obligation to give back.

Many people want to learn and work with well-respected and generous authorities, but don't always know where to find them. They may be known to their peers, or within a specific community, but have not had the opportunity to reach a wider audience. At one time, they might have submitted a proposal to the For Dummies or Chicken Soup for the Soul series of books, but it's now almost impossible to get accepted as a new author in such branded book series.

It is more than fitting that Raymond Aaron, an internationally known and respected authority in his own right, would be the one to recognize the need for a new venue in which authorities could share their considerable knowledge with readers everywhere. As the only author ever to be included in both of the book series mentioned above, Raymond has had the opportunity to give back and he understands how crucial it is for authorities to have a platform from which to share their expertise.

I

I have known and worked with Raymond for a number of years and consider him a valued friend and talented coach. He knows how to spot talented and knowledgeable people and he desires to see them prosper. Over the years, success coaching and speaking engagements around the world have made it possible for Raymond to meet many of these talented authorities. He recognizes and relates to their passion and enthusiasm for what they do, as well as their desire to share what they know. He tells me that's why he created this new nonfiction branded book series, *The Authorities*.

Dr. Nido Qubein
President, High Point University

TABLE OF CONTENTS

INTRODUCTION

Welcome to *The Authorities*. This is an anthology of ideas from individuals who have distinguished themselves in life and in business. They are authors who leave big footprints on the world, and as leaders in their particular fields, understand the importance and obligation of giving something back.

Authorities are not just experts. They are also known to be outstanding in their fields and in their communities. Because of this important difference, authorities are able to contribute more to humanity through both their chosen work and by giving back.

You will definitely know some of *The Authorities* in this book, especially since there are some world-famous ones. Others are just as exceptional, but you may not yet know about them. Our featured author, for example, is Andrea Ngui.

You have a perspective for every situation you deal with and every challenge you face. In Perspective Thinking, Andrea Ngui shares her journey of how she changed her perspective and how it impacted her life. Along the way, Andrea shares some of the challenges she personally faced, including the expectations of her family and culture, as well as chronic health concerns.

Shifting her perspective started by changing what influenced her thinking and choices. Her journey of self-discovery also involved learning to listen to her gut feelings and trusting her intuition. Andrea also identifies multiple areas where you might be sabotaging yourself, thus contributing to the feeling of being stuck.

She also shares some of the aspects of her health journey, including how she made self-care a priority in her life. Andrea's attitude changed and her world grew as a result. There are so many areas of her life that altered because of her shift in perspective and that is what she wants to gift to you.

Learn how to focus on your life goals by identifying them and laying out a timeline and milestones as you control your perspective. Andrea also shares potential obstacles to shifting your perspective, as well as how being open-minded is the key to learning and growing, thus naturally shifting your perspective. Another key that Andrea dives into is your thinking patterns and how others can influence your thinking. May this chapter serve as inspiration to you in your journey to shift your *Perspective Thinking*!

They are *The Authorities*. Learn from them. Connect with them. Let them uplift you. Learning from them and working with them is the secret ingredient for success which may well allow you to rise to the level of Authority soon. To be considered for inclusion in a subsequent edition of *The Authorities*, register to attend a future event at www.aaron.com/events where you will be interviewed and considered.

Perspective Thinking

ANDREA NGUI

Our experiences shape our perspectives. Yet, our perspectives also shape our experiences. It is a continual circle. Throughout my journey, I learned how shifting my perspective altered my experiences and opened the door to some amazing opportunities. Let me share my journey with you, as well as how shifting your perspective can help you change your life.

Often, the choices you make come down to your perspective and how it impacts your thinking. As an entrepreneur, I love the idea of breaking out of the status quo to create an amazing life. Taking that step to break my own status quo set me up to experience things and places I hadn't thought possible.

To me, the status quo is defined as settling for a corporate job, one where you spend your time making money for someone else. I have always wanted to be my own boss, but that dream had to be put on hold as I started working and gaining experience in various roles, including retail, restaurants, geographic information systems, and sales. I hopped jobs based on the money, but more importantly, I gained a lot of experience in many roles and won several awards. I focused on the material benefits, even though I wasn't focused on what type of career spoke to me.

Eventually, I realized there was more to my career than just making money. So, I asked myself what I wanted to do with the rest of my professional life.

Perhaps you have faced this situation in your own life. You know what you don't want to be doing with your career, but you haven't zeroed in on what you do want. Part of my early journey to break the status quo was understanding how my perspective influenced my thinking and my choices. I wasn't listening to my gut feelings or following my intuition. The result was that I allowed my thinking to be dominated by fears or the almighty dollar, instead of chasing my dreams. My perspective had been narrowed by the status quo that I was mindlessly following.

Things had to change as I faced some life-threatening challenges. To create the drastic change in my lifestyle, I had to start taking my health and happiness more seriously than I ever had before. One of the major challenges I live with is being seriously allergic to certain foods. I have dealt with multiple anaphylactic episodes, which meant that various jobs could expose me to life-threatening situations in a matter of moments. I needed to create a safer external environment to live in. Coping with my allergies to food isn't easy. I might as well live in bubble wrap. I could live in fear and keep myself from exploring new places and new experiences in an attempt to protect myself from everything that can harm me. It also made me realize that life can be over faster than expected. I decided to shift gears in figuring out how to start living my dream lifestyle, i.e. what makes me happy and healthy. This meant I had to gain clarity in my professional life.

Another major factor that I had to confront was chronic pain. I simply pushed myself more every day with what had to be done. I pushed my tolerance limits to the max, which meant I jeopardized my health and wellbeing. Shifting my perspective meant changing my approach. I had to figure out how to stop being overly focused on the future and, rather, focused on enjoying the present. Instead of pushing at full speed physically, I took time to relax by watching movies and listening to music. A benefit of taking this time for myself was that it also inspired my creativity.

Since so much of what I wanted was wrapped up in my health, I concentrated on that first and foremost. I visited many health practitioners, doctors, neurological clinic, conducted a CAT scan and MRI. All my results concluded my nervous system is functioning perfectly healthy. Nothing made sense. My body was constantly in pain. It was painful resting, walking, putting clothes on hangers, to swimming in the water. I found a network spinal analysis (NSA) chiropractor and increasing my physical fitness made the chronic pain permanently disappear. My chronic pain stemmed from life stressors.

I also started exercising to improve my physical endurance. Soon, I signed myself up for my first 5k and 10k road races. The benefits were not limited to physical ones. Those endorphins and the sense of accomplishment after each race spurred me to keep up my efforts.

I have also found that slowing down to take more time for self-care allows me to think with clarity. With a humbler and steadier attitude, I am no longer watching life bypass me, but instead I am enjoying life to the fullest. I am living my best lifestyle today, not later, because later may never come.

SETTING GOALS AS PART OF THE SHIFT

One of the benefits of opening my mind and heart to perspective thinking is that I listen more spiritually to the universe, using its guidance to unfold my life.

Your perspective can make you feel as if you do not have control over what is happening in your life. Professionally, you can feel as if you are a hamster on a wheel, trapped in your personal status quo. Shifting your perspective can be challenging if you are not sure what direction you truly want to go. I was so busy chasing money that I wasn't focused on achieving the right career for myself. Once I stopped dreaming and started to take action in defining my life goals and the lifestyle I wanted to live, I came to the realization of what my life profession would become.

If you meet people who have achieved their life goals and created their ideal life, they all talk about the fact that they took action. They moved! Life goals are going to set the framework for your actions and choices. Recognize that your perspective throughout life is key to staying on track to achieve what you truly desire in life.

Life is going to throw curve balls and readjusting is a necessary part of reaching your life goals. Taking the time to move at a slower pace by allocating time and space to learn from and reflect on what you have already accomplished will help you continue setting milestones that get you closer to your goals.

Identifying your life goals means that you can start laying out a timeline with milestones to help you reach your goals. Take notice of the fact that you can plan milestones forever, but if you don't start moving and take that first step, then it will just remain a to-do list with nothing crossed off and accomplished.

Start with a smaller goal, just to get moving. After all, once you achieve that first small goal, it can be all the motivation you need to tackle the next one and build resilience and consistency as you encounter setbacks. The beauty of these small steps is that even with setbacks, what you already accomplished can give you the strength, inspiration, and courage to keep moving forward. Now let's talk about some of those setbacks or obstacles, especially those that you create within yourself.

IDENTIFYING OBSTACLES TO SHIFT YOUR PERSPECTIVE

It is so easy to point the finger at your circumstances and the individuals around you as the reasons why you cannot move forward. You create reasons why you can't do something or why it is impossible. You may even blame others for your inability to accomplish your goals. The point is that those excuses and the blaming of others allows you to stay still and feel comfortable with not creating permanent change in your life. We've all heard the saying "Try, try, try again, and never give up." Perhaps giving up on your current direction by turning around into a new direction may just give you that zest feeling you long for in life. Moving forward isn't a straight line. In sports, players keep moving forward, but not always in a straight line, to get another touchdown, a basket, or a homerun.

Ask yourself, is it circumstances or an excuse that I am telling myself? Too often, our excuses block us from seeing the solutions that could be right in front of us. You need to get out of your own way. When you make excuses, you are creating barriers to dictate which way you should live.

Let's face it, self-inflicted fearmongering can be a big form of self-sabotage.

You can build up the fears in your mind to the point that you choose inaction instead of moving forward with courage.

Negative thinking can be encouraged or discouraged, depending on the thoughts you allow to be planted in your mind. You might feel like you are getting ahead, but the truth is that you are not really getting anywhere. Instead, you are simply stuck doing what you did yesterday, and if anyone points out to you that fact, then you have excuses for why you aren't progressing. You treat challenges as obstacles that cannot be overcome.

For instance, if you're dealing with a chronic health condition, you may have a tougher battle against negative thinking. After all, you are likely dealing with a variety of challenges, such as pain or limited range of motion. The physical limitations can be even harder to deal with if it impacts your independence. You can become exhausted, mentally and physically. Building a strong, healthier mindset will help you cope and potentially overcome your chronic health issue.

On the flip side, you can be the source of negative thinking for others and end up causing toxicity in someone else's thoughts. If you find yourself surrounded by those who talk negatively, stop for a moment and analyze how you are speaking. Are you drawing negativity to yourself? Shifting your perspective means being honest with yourself about the thoughts and words you allow yourself to use to describe yourself and others.

Part of changing or shifting your perspective involves power shifting your thoughts to lessen the impact of negative thinking. Once you start shifting your thinking, you will notice a breakthrough in defeating excuses and self-sabotage.

Another way to stop your negative thinking is to look at what you are feeding your brain in terms of social media. After all, there are arguments and differences of opinion that play out over the internet. You might have been in a good mood, but then you read something online and became instantly angry, even though nothing happened to you personally.

Have you ever been in a performance sports car? As the driver pushes on the gas pedal, the car can accelerate over 60 miles per hour in less than two seconds. Visualize your life performing like a sports car. If you don't push the gas pedal and tap into your power, then it is not going to perform like you anticipated. Constantly shifting your perspective as quickly as the speed of a performance sports car is key to learning what it takes to live a successful life.

Here is the important thing to remember before you can make any changes in your life. When changing your mindset, start with the invisible internal dialogue. This needs to occur before the visible external changes can properly manifest. The results of your thinking will be shown through your actions and decisions.

Your inner voice can often be one of the greatest challenges that you need to overcome to create change in your life. If you focus on thoughts based on fear, then you are going to end up becoming your own blockade. Your fear will constantly dictate what you do, trapping you in a place where you feel that everything around you is a huge risk. You could be living a fun and enjoyable life. All you need to do is conquer your fears. Always move forward with courage, even if you still feel the fear within you.

For instance, you might not like the life you are living, but it is the only one that you know. Fear might make you resist change, simply because you fear that you have so much to lose if you change. So why should you bother to make the effort? Essentially, you are self-defeating, even before you have tried or given change a chance.

Here is the reality that we all have to face. Change is coming regardless of whether we want it or not. While change can equate with loss or challenges, there is also much that can be gained.

Take a minute and look at a situation where you are fearful of change and losing what you have. Now, instead of focusing on what you might lose, let's shift to thinking about all that you might gain.

Instead of waiting for the world to bring joy and happiness into your world, start thinking about how you can create it on your own. This may include changing your routine or making a giant leap of change in your job or living situation. There are so many stories out there of individuals deciding to take a giant leap. Their experiences show how changing your thinking can allow you to make some amazing leaps in life. Your thinking can inspire you to act and make choices that align with the life you desire to live.

You need to figure out what type of life you want to live. Start focusing on what brings you joy. Often, it can be hard to separate the life that you want from the life that you are expected to live by society and your family. If you shape your life around the expectations of others, even your loved ones, then you are essentially disowning your true self for an imitation. Now, the process of letting go of those expectations and claiming the life you want to live does take effort.

How many times have you been in the position where you tried to do something and then tanked, such as a road race? Instead of crossing the finish line victoriously, you fell and twisted an ankle just a few feet past the starting line. Your perception of that experience can go one of two ways.

The first way is that you can look at that race and decide you will never run again. The second way is to look at that race and make a decision that you are going to learn from that experience. Perhaps you need different shoes, or another training regimen.

Notice that the second perspective was about finding the ways that you can learn from the experience, improve, and have a successful outcome the next time. That is a perspective that embraces learning, change, and growth. Training and practice are part of the journey.

To get to where you want to be, you need to have a clear vision of what type of life you want. Once you know where you want to be at a certain point, then you need to create an action plan around getting from point A to point B. When you create your action plan, it has to be wrapped around your perspective that it is possible to achieve.

Here is a quick exercise. Ask yourself what you tolerate from yourself that you might not tolerate in others and write it down. Remember, when you make an excuse, you are not holding yourself accountable in being true to yourself. How would you feel if you discarded things you tolerated? How would your life change?

You have to listen to your gut feelings. When you smother intuition, inertia kicks in and you get stuck with your decision making. Spend time to gain clarity with your mind to let yourself properly receive the message from your intuition.

When I was stuck in my status quo, doing the job and exhausting myself in the process, I realized that no one was going to be as concerned about my pursuit of happiness in living out my dream lifestyle than me.

No one is truly stopping you or standing in your way. The only person doing that is you! Recognize that other people will never truly understand what you need to do until you take action and they start to see the results.

Then they will understand more in-depth what you need to do and why you need to do it. Who knows? You might end up inspiring them to shift their own perspective and start creating something amazing in their own lives.

It is about designing the life you want to live. Acknowledge you deserve to live an amazing life. Become the leader of your own life destiny. Be your own hero and a role model to others.

Once I focused on creating that lifestyle which I had designed for myself, then I started to live the best years of my life. The radiant self-fulfilling lifestyle journey that I began creating for myself has been the most wonderful and marvelous experience, and I get to experience it every single day. The amount of peace and harmony that I know is so abundant. It motivates me to continue to achieve and focus on living this lifestyle that I desire and deserve to live. What you prioritize is what your life will reflect, so make sure you are prioritizing the things that bring you joy and happiness.

Everything that I have achieved started with changing my perspective and focusing on what was possible instead of labeling it as impossible. Now let's focus on how shifting your perspective can help improve your relationships with others.

CREATING AMAZING RELATIONSHIPS IN YOUR LIFE

Relationships with individuals throughout your life are going to be complicated. You may find that someone challenges you, while another person provides unconditional support. As you are making amazing changes and shifts in your life, you need to shape your personal inner circle to find those who will challenge you and support you, even as you do the same for them.

Think about the people who surround you now. Do they support you on your journey of growth? Do they hold you accountable when you start to slip back into the status quo or that old way of thinking and behaving? If you want to create a major shift in your life, then you need those individuals to hold you accountable and to be honest with you.

Staying true to ourselves morally and ethically is not always easy when we surround ourselves with those who do not subscribe to our morals and ethics. Those within your inner circle are going to have the most profound impact on your thinking and actions.

As part of your journey to building your inner circle, it is important to clarify what you want to achieve in your life. Remember to focus on yourself. The best relationship, the best friendship you have, is the relationship you have with yourself. Self-mastery is key in figuring out how to live a purposeful life.

I embraced my dreams by initially writing them down. For example, I purchased my first home on my own, took a trip to Machu Picchu and the Galapagos Islands, and revolved my schedule around volunteering at events I always wanted to partake in. I achieved these dreams, but the timeframe was a lot longer than predicted.

Where do you want to go? What do you want to see and experience? The world is large and there are plenty of places to see, cultures to explore and experience, and food to try. Another benefit of traveling is that you build confidence in your abilities, be it to navigate travelling in a foreign country or conquering a mountain. Start crossing things off your bucket list or else you'll find yourself with a long list that was never accomplished.

Be open to new experiences and allow yourself to enjoy a variety of what life has to offer. It's the best way to truly discover yourself. It's time to stop existing and start living a fun and enjoyable life. When you purposefully plan the type of life you want and share with the world how you want to be treated, then people will respond.

Take a piece of paper and spend a few minutes thinking about everything that you want to accomplish in your life. Don't put timeframes on it. Goals and milestones move you forward in your life and can help you achieve what is necessary to transition through different life stages. A bucket list is based around experiences and moments that you want to have as part of your life's journey.

CREATE FINANCIAL INDEPENDENCE

Another part of perspective thinking is homeownership. Some individuals have different ideas regarding owning property, but the truth is that homeownership is key to building your net worth.

Financially, I had to be frugal to accomplish my goals of becoming an entrepreneur and homeowner. When you have a greater purpose, a greater "why" for your shift in perspective, and a greater reason why you are doing what you are doing, then everything else becomes irrelevant.

Being worried about money and driven to make more can lead to an obsession at the level that you will ignore your loved ones, your health, and your well-being. I did exactly that, constantly burnt out to prove that I could make it in the corporate world. Keeping up an image that I didn't want to be known for.

You can move yourself forward financially if you take responsibility for your choices and take control of how you are using your assets. If it seems as if you are sabotaging yourself financially, then you might want to stop and explore your attitude regarding money. Often, your struggles to stay on budget, control your spending, or save to invest can be wrapped up in beliefs about money that have burrowed into your subconscious and become part of the spending choices you make on a daily basis.

The way money and financial matters were presented when you were younger impacts your financial perspective today. The last financial recession had a major impact on many families and their finances. For the people this affected, their goal now may be to take fewer financial risks to avoid having that experience happen to them again.

If you look back to those who grew up during the Great Depression, they often struggled to spend money on anything, even when they clearly needed it. These individuals had lived through traumatic financial experiences, so their future choices of not wanting to put money in banks or to live very frugally were understandable. If your grandparents were raised in that era, they may have passed some of those beliefs or fears onto you.

What are your beliefs about money? How you view money and the beliefs behind those views will help you to appreciate why you make certain financial decisions. If you don't figure out the underlying cause, you will be unable to fix it. Instead, you will simply manage the symptoms, which is not the best long-term solution.

THE POWER IN WRITING

Throughout this chapter, you have learned the value in shifting your perspective. There are many fantastic opportunities in life if you explore with curiosity.

It is possible to heal from the past and move confidently into your future. Find ways to move, act, and create motion within your life. Working with a life coach can support you in your self-discovery journey. I help both men and women who are fitness enthusiasts and business owners to achieve their goals by focusing on successful habits, mindsets, wellbeing, nutrition, fitness, and relationships. I want to tell you that it is possible to heal from the past and live a better life starting today. You deserve to live your dream lifestyle now. Contact Andrea Ngui at www.herovi.coach.

Start by creating steppingstones to put yourself in a position to leap into the life you always wanted to live. Intention and deliberate actions are key to shifting your perspective.

Let's put perspective thinking into perspective. For example, whether it's a testimonial on LinkedIn, feedback on a report, a critique of a movie, a biography for a speaking engagement, or an opinion of a product on Amazon, they usually all have a more thoroughly written response than a verbal response. You know what I am saying?

Articulating your message by writing it down, or typing it out, has a profound effect on your level of perspective thinking. It helps heighten your level of awareness, level of learning, level of maturity, and level of wisdom. So, will you be writing things down on paper or on an electronic device?

Social media platforms are great tools in training your brain to ensure you are as articulate as possible with your message. Your message should be clear and concise with the knowledge you want others to read. You want to minimize the range of misinterpretation.

When it comes to complex things in life, how can you figure things out if you can't even articulate yourself proficiently by initially writing them down?

Don't get hung up on the agonizingly annoying feeling that the process will take too long. The length of time is irrelevant. Doing a half fast job leaves you stuck in a repetitive loophole with the illusion of the falsehood that you solved the issue. Writing it down and writing it out allows you to organize your thoughts. How can you expect to communicate clearly if you don't truly and entirely know what you want to say?

Expressing yourself by articulating your feelings with better words will help you get from where you are now to where you want to be. Eventually, it will help you create what you desire to achieve in life.

Creativity can be taught through perspective thinking. The television show Stranger Things has an upside-down world, which is another dimension of the universe. Songs, movies, quotes, clichés, and poetry all tend to have a deeper meaning than what the eye beholds on the surface. Has it ever happened to you when, over time, hearing the same clichés makes a new insight pop into your head? You start to wonder, "How did I miss that this entire time? I didn't know. I had no idea. Why didn't you tell me before?" Seeing things from another angle, from the inside out, and elevating your level of thinking helps you improve in becoming a problem solver within your own life.

Preparation is key in achieving the result of success. As Eric Thomas, aka ET, says, "Fall in love with the process, and the results will come." Practice makes perfect. Do the training, drills, exercises, practices, and show up where you really need to grind it out.

Is this why athletes practice so much? To fine tune their athleticism? Could this be a success method in how people accomplish so much in a day? A successful habit to develop is to intentionally think about embracing a continuous higher level of awareness with everything. It all starts with your level of perspective thinking. Life will start to unfold with what you deserve, and you will reap what you sow. Let this glimpse into how I shifted my perspective inspire you to do the same.

Contact Andrea Ngui at **www.herovi.coach** to learn how you can work together as you shift your perspective thinking and grow your business and personal lifestyle.

Step Into Greatness

LES BROWN

You have greatness within you. You can do more than you could ever imagine. The problem most people have is that they set a goal and then ask "how can I do it? I don't have the necessary skills or education or experience".

I know what that's like. I wasted 14 years on asking myself how I could be a motivational speaker. My mind focused on the negative—on the things that were in my way, rather than on the things that were not.

It's not what you don't have but what you think you need that keeps you from getting what you want from life. But, when the dream is big enough, the obstacles don't matter. You'll get there if you stay the course. Nothing can stop you but death itself.

Think about that last statement for a minute. There's nothing on this earth that can stop you from achieving what it is that you want. So, get out of your way, and quit sabotaging your dreams. Do everything in your power to make them happen—because you cannot fail!

They say the best way to die is with your loved ones gathered around your bed. But what if you were dying and it was the ideas you never acted upon, the gifts you never used and the dreams you never pursued, that were circled around your bed? Answer that question right now. Write down your answers. If you die this very moment what ideas, what gifts, what dreams will die with you?

Then say: I refuse to die an unlived life! You beat out 40 million sperm to get here, and you'll never have to face such odds again. Walk through the field of life and leave a trail behind.

One day, one of my rich friends brought my mother a new pair of shoes for me. Now, even though we weren't well off, I didn't want them; they were a size nine and I was a size nine and a half. My mother didn't listen and told my sister to go get some Vaseline, which she rubbed all over my feet. Then my mother had me put those shoes on, minding that I didn't scrunch down the heel. She had my sister run some water in the bathtub, and I was told to get in and walk around in the water. I said that my feet hurt. She just ignored me and asked about my day at school, how everything went and did I get into any fights? I knew what she was up to, that she was trying to distract me, so I said I had only gotten into three fights. After a while mother asked me if my feet still hurt. I admitted that the pain had indeed lessened. She kept me walking in that tub until I had a brand new pair of comfortable, size nine and a half shoes.

You see, once the leather in the shoes got wet, they stretched! And what you need to do is stretch a little. I believe that most people don't set high goals and miss them, but rather, they set lower goals and hit them and then they stay there, stuck on the side of the highway of life. When you're pursuing your greatness, you don't know what your limitations are, and you need to act like you don't have any. If you shoot for the moon and miss, you'll still be in the stars.

You also need coaching (a mentor). Why? There are times you, too, will find yourself parked on the side of the highway of life with no gas in the vehicle. What you need then is someone to stop and offer to pick up some gas down the road a ways and bring it back to you. That person is your coach. Yes, they are there for advice, but their main job is to help you through the difficulties that life throws at all of us.

Another reason for having a coach is that you can't see the picture when you're in the frame. In other words, he or she can often see where you are with a clarity and focus that's unavailable to you. They're not going to leave you parked along the road of life, nor are they going to allow you to be stuck in the moment like a photo in a frame.

And let's say you just can't see you're way forward. You don't believe it's possible. Sometimes you just have to believe in someone's belief in you. This could be your coach, a loved one or even a staunch friend. You need to hear them say you can do it, time and again. Because, after all, faith comes from hearing and hearing and hearing.

Look at it this way. Most people fail because of possibility blindness. They can't see what lies before them. There are always possibilities. Because of this, your dream is possible. You may fail often. In fact, I want you to say this: I will fail my way to success. Here is why.

I had a TV show that failed. I felt I had to go back to public speaking. I had failed, so I parked my car for ten years. Then I saw Dr. Wayne Dyer was still on PBS and I decided to call them. They said they would love to work with me and asked where I had been. I wasn't as good as I had been ten years before, as I was out of practice, but I still had to get back in the game. I was determined to drive on empty.

Listen to recordings, go to seminars, challenge yourself, and you'll begin to step into your greatness, you'll begin to fill yourself with the energy you need to climb to ever greater heights. Most people never attend a seminar. They won't invest money in books or audio programs. You put yourself in the top 5 percent just by making a different choice than the average person. This is called contrary thinking. It's a concept taken from the financial industry. One considers choosing the exact opposite behaviour of the average person as a way to get better than average results. You don't have to make the contrarian choice, but if you don't have anything to lose by going that road, why not consider the option?

Make your move before you're ready. Walk by faith not by sight and make sure you're happy doing it. If you can't be happy, what else is there? Helen Keller said, "Life is short, eat the dessert first."

What is faith? Many of us think of God when we think of faith. A different viewpoint claims that faith is a firm belief in something for which there is no proof. I would rather think of faith as something that is believed especially with strong conviction. It is this last definition I am referring to when I say walk by faith not by sight. Be happy and go forth with strong conviction that you are destined for greatness.

An important step on your way to greatness is to take the time to detoxify. You've got to look at the people in your life. What are they doing for you? Are they setting a pace that you can follow? If not, whose pace have you adjusted to? If you're the smartest in your group, find a new group.

Are the people in your life pulling you down or lifting you up? You know what to do, right? Banish the negative and stay with the positive; it's that simple. Dr. Norman Vincent Peale once said (when I was in the audience), "You are special. You have greatness within you, and you can do more than you could ever possibly imagine."

He overrode the inner conversations in my mind and reached the heart of me. He set me on fire. This is yet another reason for seeking out the help of a coach or mentor or other new people in your life. They can do what Dr. Peale did for me. They can set your passion free.

How important is it to have the right kind of person/people on your side? There was a study done that determined it takes 16 people saying you can do something to overcome one person who says you can't do something. That's right, one negative, unsupportive person can wipe out the work of 16 other supportive people. The message can't be any clearer than that.

Let's face the cold, hard truth: most people stay in park along the highway of life. They never feel the passion, the love for their fellow man, or for the work they do. They are stuck in the proverbial rut. What's the reason? There are many reasons, but only one common factor: fear — fear of change, fear of failure, fear of success, fear they may not be good enough, fear of competition, even fear of rejection.

"Rejection is a myth," says Jack Canfield, co-author of The Chicken Soup for the Soul series. "It's not like you get a slap in the face each time you are rejected." Why not take every "no" you receive as a vitamin, and every time you take one know you are another step closer to success.

You will win if you don't quit. Even a broken clock is right twice a day.

Professional baseball players, on average, get on base just three times out of every ten times they face the opposing pitcher. Even superstars fail half of the time they appear at the plate.

Top commissioned salespeople face similar odds. They may make one sale from every three people they see, but it will have taken them between 75 and 100 telephone calls to make the 15 appointments they need to close their five sales for the week. And these are statistics for the elite. Most salespeople never reach these kinds of numbers.

People don't spend their lives working for just one company anymore. This means you must build up a set of skills and experiences that are portable. This can be done a number of ways, but my favourite approaches follow.

You must be willing to do the things others won't do in order to have tomorrow the things that others don't have. Provide more service than you get paid for. Set some high standards for yourself.

Begin each day with your most difficult task. The rest of the day will seem more enjoyable and a whole lot easier.

Someone needs help with a problem? Be the solution to that problem.

Also, find those tasks that are being consistently ignored and do them. You'll be surprised by the results. An acquaintance of mine used this approach at a number of entry-level positions and each time he quickly ended up being offered a position in management.

You must increase your energy. Kick it up a notch. We are spirits having a physical existence; let your spirit shine. Quit frittering away your energy. Use it to move you closer to the achievement of your dreams. Refuse to spend it on non-productive activities.

What do people say about you when you leave a room? Are you willing to take responsibility—to walk your talk. There is a terrible epidemic sweeping our nation, and it is the refusal to take responsibility for one's actions. Consider that at some point in any situation there will have been a moment where you could have done something to change the outcome. To that end you are responsible for what happened. It's a hard thing to accept, but it's true.

Life's hard. It was hard when I was told I had cancer. I had sunken into despair, and was hiding away in my study when my son came in. My son asked me if I was going to die. What could I do? I told him I was going to fight, even though I was scared. I also told him that I needed some help. Not because I was weak but because I wanted to stay strong. Keep asking until you get help. Don't stop until you get it.

A setback is the setup for a comeback. A setback is simply a misstep on the long road of success. It means nothing in the larger scheme of things. And, surprisingly, it sets you up for your next win. It tends to focus you and your energy on your immediate goals, paving the way for your next sprint, for your comeback.

It's worth it. Your dreams are worth the sacrifices you'll have to make to achieve them. Find five reasons that will make your dreams worth it for you. Say to yourself, I refuse to live an unlived life.

If you are casual about your dreams, you'll end up a casualty. You must be passionate about your dreams, living and breathing them throughout your days. You've got to be hungry! People who are hungry refuse to take no for an answer. Make NO your vitamin. Be unstoppable. Be hungry.

Let me give you an example of what I mean by hungry …

I decided I wanted to become a disc jockey, so I went down to the local radio station and asked the manager, Mr. Milton "Butterball" Smith, if he had a job available for a disc jockey. He said he did not. The next day I went back, and Mr. Smith asked "Weren't you here yesterday?" I explained that I was just checking to see if anyone was sick or had died. He responded by telling me not to come back again. Day three, I went back again—with the same story. Mr. Smith told me to get out of there. I came back the fourth day and gave Mr. Smith my story one more time. He was so beside himself that he told me to get him a cup of coffee. I said, "Yes, sir!" That's how I became the errand boy.

While working as an errand boy at the station, I took every opportunity to hang out with the deejays and to observe them working. After I had taught myself how to run the control room, it was just a matter of biding my time.

Then one day an opportunity presented itself. One of the disc jockeys by the name of Rockin' Roger was drinking heavily while he was on the air. It was a Saturday afternoon. And there I was, the only one there.

I watched him through the control-room window. I walked back and forth in front of that window like a cat watching a mouse, saying "Drink, Rock, Drink!" I was young. I was ready. And I was hungry.

Pretty soon, the phone rang. It was the station manager. He said, "Les, this is Mr. Klein."

I said, "Yes, I know."

He said, "Rock can't finish his program."

I said, "Yes sir, I know."

He said, "Would you call one of the other disc jockeys to fill in?"

I said, "Yes sir, I sure will, sir."

And when he hung up, I said, "Now he must think I'm crazy." I called up my mama and my girlfriend, Cassandra, and I told them, "Ya'll go out on the front porch and turn up the radio, I'M ABOUT TO COME ON THE AIR!"

I waited 15 or 20 minutes and called the station manager back. I said, "Mr. Klein, I can't find NOBODY!"

He said, "Young boy, do you know how to work the controls?"

I said, "Yes, sir."

He said, "Go in there, but don't say anything. Hear me?"

I said, "Yes, sir."

I couldn't wait to get old Rock out of the way. I went in there, took my seat behind that turntable, flipped on the microphone and let 'er rip.

"Look out, this is me, LB., triple P. Les Brown your platter-playin' papa. There were none before me and there will be none after me, therefore that makes me the one and only. Young and single and love to mingle, certified, bona fide and indubitably qualified to bring you satisfaction and a whole lot of action. Look out baby, I'm your LOVE man."

I WAS HUNGRY!

During my adult life I've been a deejay, a radio station manager, a Democrat in the Ohio Legislature, a minister, a TV personality, an author and a public speaker, but I've always looked after what I valued most—my mother. What I want for her is one of my dreams, one of my goals.

My life has been a true testament to the power of positive thinking and the infinite human potential. I was born in an abandoned building on a floor in Liberty City, a low-income section of Miami, Florida, and adopted at six weeks of age by Mrs. Mamie Brown, a 38-year-old single woman, cafeteria cook and domestic worker. She had very little education or financial means, but a very big heart and the desire to care for myself and my twin brother. I call myself Mrs. Mamie Brown's Baby Boy and I say that all that I am and all that I ever hoped to be, I owe to my mother.

My determination and persistence in searching for ways to help my mother overcome poverty and developing my philosophy to do whatever it takes to achieve success led me to become a distinguished authority on harnessing human potential and success. That philosophy is best expressed by the following …

"If you want a thing bad enough to go out and fight for it,
to work day and night for it,
to give up your time, your peace and your sleep for it…
if all that you dream and scheme is about it,
and life seems useless and worthless without it…
if you gladly sweat for it and fret for it and plan for it
and lose all your terror of the opposition for it…
if you simply go after that thing you want
with all of your capacity, strength and sagacity,
faith, hope and confidence and stern pertinacity…
if neither cold, poverty, famine, nor gout,
sickness nor pain, of body and brain,
can keep you away from the thing that you want…
if dogged and grim you beseech and beset it,
with the help of God, you will get it!"

Branding
Small Business

RAYMOND AARON

B randing is an incredibly important tool for creating and building your business. Large companies have been benefiting from branding ever since people first started selling things to other people. Branding made those businesses big.

If you're a small business owner, you probably imagine that small companies are different and don't need branding as much as large companies do. Not true. The truth is small businesses need branding just as much, if not more, than large companies.

Perhaps you've thought about branding, but assumed you'd need millions of dollars to do it properly, or that branding is just the same thing as marketing. Nothing could be further from the truth.

Marketing is the engine of your company's success. Branding is the fuel in that engine.

In the old days, salespeople were a big part of the selling process. They recommended one product over another and laid out the reasons why it was better. Salespeople had credibility because they knew about all the products, and customers often took the advice they had to offer.

Today, consumers control the buying process. They shop in big box stores, super-sized supermarkets, and over the Internet — where there are no salespeople. Buyers now get online and gather information beforehand. They learn about all the products available and look to see if there really is any difference between them. Consumers also read reviews and check social media to see if both the company and the product are reputable. In other words, they want to know what the brand is all about.

The way of commerce used to be: "Nothing happens till something is sold." Today it's: "Nothing happens till something is branded!"

DEFINING A BRAND

A brand is a proper name that stands for something. It lives in the consumer's mind, has positive or negative characteristics, and invokes a feeling or an image. In short, it's a person's perception of a product or a company.

When all goes well, consumers associate the same characteristics with a brand that the company talks about in its advertising, public relations, marketing and sales materials. Of course, when a product doesn't live up to what the company says about it, the brand gets a bad reputation. On the other hand, if a product or service over-delivers on the promises made, the brand can become a superstar.

RECOGNIZING BRANDING AND ITS CHARACTERISTICS

Branding is the science and art of making something that isn't unique, unique. Branding in the marketplace is the same as branding on a ranch. On a ranch, ranchers use branding to differentiate their cattle from every other rancher's cattle (because all cattle look pretty much the same). In the marketplace, branding is what makes a product stand out in a crowd of similar products. The right branding gets you noticed, remembered and sold — or perhaps I should say bought, because today it is all about buying, not selling.

There are four main characteristics of branding that make it an integral part of the marketing and purchasing process.

1. Branding makes you trustworthy and known

Branding makes a product more special than other products. With branding, a normal, everyday product has a personality, and a first and last name, and people know who you are.

In today's marketplace, most products are, more or less, just like their competition. Toilet paper is toilet paper, milk is milk, and a grocery store by any other name is still a grocery store. However, branding takes a product and makes it unique. For example, high-quality drinking water is available from just about every tap in the Western world and it's free, but people pay good money for it when it comes in a bottle. Branding takes bottled water and makes Evian.

Furthermore, every aspect of your brand gives potential customers a feeling or comfort level that they associate with you. The more powerful and positive that feeling is, the more easily and more frequently they will want to do business with you and, indeed, will do business with you.

2. Branding differentiates you from others

Strong branding makes you better than your competition, and makes your product name memorable and easy to remember. Even if your product is absolutely the same as every other product like it, branding makes it special. Branding makes it the first product a consumer thinks about when deciding to make a purchase.

Branding also makes a product seem popular. Everyone knows about it, which implicitly says people like it. And, if people like it, it must be good.

3. Branding makes you worth more money

The stronger your branding is, the more likely people are willing to spend that little bit extra because they believe you, your product, your service, or your business are worth it. They may say they won't, but they will. They do it all the time.

For example, a one-pound box of Godiva chocolates costs about $40; the same weight of Hershey's Kisses costs about $4. The quality of the chocolate isn't ten times greater. The reason people buy Godiva is that the brand Godiva means "gift" whereas the brand Hershey means "snack". Gifts obviously cost more than snacks.

4. Branding pre-sells your product

In the buying age, people most often make the decision on which products to pick up before they walk into the store. The stronger the branding, the more likely people are to think in terms of your product rather than the product category. For example, people are as likely, maybe even more likely, to add Hellmann's to the shopping list as they are to write down simply mayo. The same is true for soda, ketchup, and many other products with successful, strong branding.

Plus, as soon as a shopper gets to the shelf, branding can provide a quick reminder of what products to grab in a few ways:

- An icon or logo
- A specific color
- An audio icon

BRANDING IN A SMALL BUSINESS

Big companies spend millions of dollars on advertising, marketing, and public relations (PR) to build recognition of a new product name. They get their selling messages out to the public using television, radio, magazines, and the Internet. They can even throw money at damage control when necessary. The strategies for branding are the same in a small business, but the scale, costs, and a few of the tactics change.

Make your brand name work harder

The name of a small business can mean everything in terms of branding. Your brand name needs to work harder for your business than you do. It's the first thing a prospective customer sees, and it is how they will remember you. A brand name has to be memorable when spoken, and focused in its meaning. If the name doesn't represent what consumers believe about a product and the company that makes it, then that brand will fail.

In building your product's reputation and image, less is often significantly more. Make sure the name you choose immediately gives a sense of what you do.

Large corporations have millions of dollars to take a meaningless brand name and make it stand for something. Small businesses don't, so use words that really mean something. Strive for something interesting and be right on point. You don't need to be boring.

Plumbers, for example, would do well setting themselves apart with names like "The On-Time Plumber" or "24/7 Plumbing". The same is true for electricians, IT providers, or even marketing consultants. Plenty of other types of business are so general in nature they just don't work hard enough in a business or product name.

Even the playing field: The Net

The Internet has leveled the playing field for small businesses like nothing else. You can use the Internet in several ways to market your brand:

Website: Developing and maintaining a website is easier than ever. Anyone can find your business regardless of its size.

Social Media: Facebook and Twitter can promote your brand in a cost-effective manner.

BUILDING YOUR BRAND WITH THE BRANDING LADDER

Even if you do everything perfectly the first time (and I don't know anyone who does), branding takes time. How much time isn't just up to you, but you can speed things along by understanding the different levels of branding, as well as the business and marketing strategies that can get you to the top.

Introducing the Branding Ladder

Moving through the levels of branding is like climbing a ladder to the top of the marketplace. The Branding Ladder has five distinct rungs and, unlike stairs, you can't take them two at a time. You have to take them in order, and some businesses spend more time on each rung than others.

You can also think of the Branding Ladder in terms of a scale from zero to ten. Everyone starts at zero. If you properly climb the ladder, you can end up at 12 out of 10. The Branding Ladder below shows a special rung at the top of the ladder that can take your business over the top. The following section explains the Branding Ladder and how your small business can move up it.

THE BRANDING LADDER	
Brand Advocacy	12/10
Brand Insistence	10/10
Brand Preference	3/10
Brand Awareness	1/10
Brand Absence	0/10

Rung 1: Living in the void

Your business, in fact every business, starts at the bottom rung, which is called brand absence, meaning you have no brand whatsoever except your own name. On a scale of one to ten, brand absence is, of course, zero. That's the worst place to live and obviously the most difficult entrepreneurially. The good news is that the only way is up.

Ninety-seven percent of businesses live on this rung of the Branding Ladder. They earn far less than they want to earn, far less than they should earn, and far less than they would earn if they did exactly the same work under a real brand.

Rung 2: Achieving awareness

Brand awareness is a good first step up the ladder to the second rung. Actually, it's really good, especially because 97 percent of businesses never get there. You want people to be aware of you. When person A speaks to person B and says, "Have you heard of "The 24/7 Plumber?" You want the answer to be "yes".

On that scale of one to ten, however, brand awareness is only a one. It's better than nothing, but not that much better. Although people know of your brand, being aware doesn't mean that they are interested in buying it. Coca Cola drinkers know about Pepsi, but they don't drink it.

Rung 3: Becoming the preferred brand

Getting to the third rung, brand preference, is definitely a real step up. This rung means that people prefer to use your product or service rather than that of your competition. They believe there is a real difference between you and others, and you're their first choice. This rung is a crucial branding stage for parity products, such as bottled water and breakfast cereals, not to mention plumbers, electricians, lawyers, and all the others. Brand preference is clearly better than brand awareness, but it's less than halfway up the ladder.

Car rental companies represent a perfect example of why brand preference may not be enough. When someone lands at an airport and needs to rent a car on the spot, he or she may go straight to the preferred rental counter. If that company has a car available, it's a sale. However, if all the cars for that company have been rented, the person will move to the next rental kiosk without much thought, because one rental car is just as good as another.

Exerting Brand Preference needs to be easy and convenient

If all you have is brand preference, your business is on shaky ground and you can lose business for the feeblest of reasons. Very few people go to a second or third supermarket just to find their favorite brand of bottled water. Similarly, a shopper may prefer one store over another but, if both stores sell the same products, he or she will often go to the closest store even if it is not the better liked one. The reason for staying nearby does not need to be a dramatic one — the shopper may simply be tired, on a tight schedule, or not in the mood to travel.

Rung 4: Making it you and only you

When your customers are so committed to your product or service that they won't accept a substitute, you have reached the fourth rung of the Branding Ladder. All companies strive to reach this place, called brand insistence.

Brand insistence means that someone's experience with a product in terms of performance, durability, customer service, and image has been sufficiently exceptional. As a result, the product has earned an incredible level of loyalty. If the product isn't available where the customer is, he or she will literally not buy something else. Rather, the person will look for the preferred product elsewhere. Can you imagine what a fabulous place this is for a company to be? Brand insistence is the best of the best, the perfect ten out of ten, the whole ball of wax.

Apple is a perfect example of brand insistence

Apple users don't just think, they know in their heads and hearts, that anything made by Apple is technologically-advanced, user-friendly, and just all-around superior. Committed to everything Apple, Mac users won't even entertain the thought that a PC may have positive attributes.

Apple people love everything about their Macs, iPads, iPhones, the Mac stores and all those apps. When the company introduces a new product, many of its brand-insistent fans actually wait in line overnight to be one of the first to have it. Steve Jobs is one of their idols.

Considering one big potential problem

Unfortunately, you can lose brand insistence much more quickly than you can achieve it. Brand-insistent customers have such high expectations that they can be disillusioned or disappointed by just one bad product experience. You also have to consistently reinforce the positives because insistence can fade over time. Even someone who has bought and re-bought a specific brand of car for the last 20 years can decide it's just time for a change. That's how fickle the world is.

At ten out of ten, brand insistence may seem like the top rung of the ladder, but it's not. One rung is actually better, and it involves getting your brand-insistent customers to keep polishing your brand for you.

Rung 5: Getting customers to do the work for you

Brand advocacy is the highest rung on the ladder. It's better than ten out of ten because you have customers who are so happy with your product that they want everyone to know about it and use it. Think of them as uber-fans. Not only do they recommend you to friends and family, they also practically shout your praises from the rooftops, interrupt conversations among strangers to give their opinion, and tell everyone they meet how fantastic you are. Most companies can only aspire to this level of customer satisfaction. Apple is one of the few large corporations in recent history that has brand advocates all over the world.

- Brand advocacy does the following five extraordinary things for your company. Brand advocacy:

- Provides a level of visibility that you couldn't pay for if you tried. Brand advocates are so enthusiastic they talk about you all the time, and reach people in ways general media and public relations can't. You get great visibility because they make sure people actually listen.

- Delivers free advertising and public relations. Companies love the extra super-positive messaging, all for free.

- Affords a level of credibility that literally can't be bought. Brand advocates are more than just walking testimonials. They are living proof that you are the best.

- Provides pre-sold prospective customers. Advocate recommendations carry so much weight that they are worth much more than plain referrals. They deliver customers ready and committed to purchasing your product or service.

- Increases profits exponentially. Brand advocates are money-making machines for your business because they increase sales and decrease marketing costs.

For these reasons, brand advocacy is 12 out of 10!!

BRANDING YOURSELF:
HOW TO DO SO IN FOUR EASY WAYS

If you're interested in branding your product or company, you may not be sure where to begin. The good news: I'm here to help. You can brand in many ways, but here I pare it down to four ways to help you start:

Branding by association

This way involves hanging out with and being seen with people who are very much higher than you in your particular niche.

Branding by achievement

This way repurposes your previous achievements.

Branding by testimonial

This way makes use of the testimonials that you receive but have likely never used.

Branding by WOW

A WOW is the pleasantly unexpected, the equivalent of going the extra mile. The easiest and most certain way to WOW people is to tell them that you've written a book. To discover how you can write a book, go to www.BrandingSmallBusinessForDummies.com.

Sex, Love and Relationships

DR. JOHN GRAY

Just as great sex is important to lasting love, good health is important to sex and relationships. About 12 years ago, I cured myself of early stage Parkinson's disease. The doctors were amazed, but my wife was even more amazed. She noted that our relationship and sex life had become dramatically better. It turns out that the natural supplements I used to reverse Parkinson's can also make you more attentive and loving in your relationship. At that point, I realized that good relationship skills alone were not enough to sustain love and passion for a lifetime.

I shared many insights gained from my 40 years' experience as a marriage counselor and coach in *Men Are From Mars, Women Are From Venus*. And while my insights go a long way towards helping men and women understand and support each other, good communication skills alone are not always enough. For better relationships, we not only need to be healthy, but we must also experience optimum brain function.

If you are tired, depressed, anxious, not sleeping well, or in pain, then certainly romantic feelings will become a thing of the past. My recovery from Parkinson's revealed to me the profound connection between the quality of our health and our relationships. This insight has motivated me, over the past twelve years, to research the secrets of optimum health as a foundation for lasting love.

These are health secrets that are generally not explored in medical school. In medical school, doctors are indoctrinated into the culture of examining the symptoms, identifying the sickness, and prescribing a drug to treat that sickness. They learn very little about how to be healthy or to sustain successful relationships.

There are no university courses entitled "Better Nutrition For Better Sex". Drugs sometimes save lives, but they also have negative side effects that do little to preserve the passion in a relationship. Ideally, drugs should be used as a last resort and 90 % of our health plan should be drug free. From this perspective, the heath care crisis, as well as our high rate of divorce in America, is indirectly caused by our dependence on doctors and prescription drugs.

Most people have not even considered that taking prescribed drugs (even for the small stuff) can weaken their relationships, which in turn makes them more vulnerable to more disease. For example, if you are feeling depressed or anxious, a drug may numb your pain, but it does nothing to help you correct the cause of your problem. It can even prevent you from feeling your natural motivation to get the emotional support you need. In a variety of ways, our common health complaints are all expressions of two major conditions: our lack of education to identify and support unmet gender-specific emotional needs; and our lack of education to identify and support unmet gender-specific nutritional needs.

With an understanding of natural solutions that have been around for thousands of years, drugs are not needed to treat many common complaints. Some symptoms like low energy, weight gain, allergies, hormonal imbalance, mood swings, poor sleep, indigestion, lack of focus, ADD and ADHD, procrastination, low motivation, memory loss, decreased libido, PMS, vaginal dryness, muscle and joint pain, or the lack of passion in life and/or our relationships can be treated drug-free. By using drugs (even over-the-counter drugs) to treat these common complaints, our bodies and relationships are weakened, making us more vulnerable to bigger and more costly health challenges like cancer, diabetes, heart disease, auto-immune disease, dementia, and Alzheimer's. In simple terms, by handling the easy stuff (the common complaints) without doctors and drugs, we can protect ourselves from the big stuff (cancer, heart disease, dementia, etc.) We can be healthy and also enjoy lasting love and passion in our personal lives.

Even if you are taking anti-depressants or hormone replacement therapy, sometimes all it takes to stop treating the symptom is to directly handle the cause. With specific mineral orotates (something most people have never heard of) or omega three oil from the brains of salmon, your stress levels immediately drop and you begin to feel happy and in love again.

For every health challenge, we have explored the effects on our relationships, with as well as natural remedies that can sometimes produce immediate positive results. You can find these natural solutions to common health complaints for free at my website: www.MarsVenus.com.

What they don't teach in medical school is how to be healthy and happy without the use of drugs or hormone replacement. By refusing drugs and taking responsibility for your health, a wealth of new possibilities can become available to you. We are designed to be healthy and happy, and it is within our reach if we commit to increasing our knowledge.

New research regarding the brain differences in men and women reveals how specific nutritional supplements, combined with gender-specific relationship and self-nurturing skills, can stimulate the hormones of health, happiness and increased energy. Over the past 10 years in my healing center in California, I witnessed how natural solutions coupled with gender-specific relationship skills could solve our common health complaints without drugs. By addressing these common complaints without prescribed drugs, not only do we feel better, but our relationships have the potential to improve dramatically.

Ultimately the cause of all our common complaints is higher stress levels. Researchers around the world all agree that chronic stress levels in our bodies provide a basis for any and all disease to take hold. An easy and quick solution for lowering our stress reactions is specific nutritional support combined with gender-smart relationship skills. Extra nutritional support is needed because stress depletes the body very quickly of essential nutrients. When a car engine is running more quickly, it uses fuel more quickly. When we are stressed, we need both extra nutrients and extra emotional support. Understanding what we need to take and where to get it requires education. Every week day at www.MarsVenus.com I have a live daily show where I freely answer questions and provide this much-needed new gender-specific insight.

At www.MarsVenus.com, we are happy to share what we have learned for creating healthy bodies and positive relationships. You can find a host of natural solutions for common complaints and feel confident that you have the power to feel fully alive with an abundance of energy and positive feelings that will enrich all your relationships.

The Mindset of Success

ANNA GRIFFIN

My mother said something to me once that has stuck in my mind ever since, and that is, "Conviction and comfort don't live in the same block." If you want your life to be fulfilling and continually reach your goals and dreams, then there are going to be times of discomfort and overcoming fear.

When I started writing this chapter, I was completely filled with fear, uncertainty, and confusion. I guess it was fear of having my thoughts heard, and thinking, "Who am I to say all this?" or "What will others say?" These types of thoughts and questions often accompany us in moments when we least want it or expect it. "Am I strong enough?" "Am I going to be accepted and will I fit in?" are our common thoughts. But quickly enough I thought to myself, "Well, what's the worst thing that is going to happen?" I set myself back on track to have the right mindset and to think of the many exceptional leaders I have been fortunate to work for throughout my career and travels.

I've made it my mission to understand their exceptional attributes, which served them in moments of fear and self-doubt. But it is not always about the tools that are being used, the business models or the frameworks. Often, it is more about their mindset and leadership and what kind of people we become in their presence.

Living in many countries and getting to know different cultures, from the West to the East, I have had the privilege to better understand what makes a person successful, happy, and someone you would want to follow as a business leader, or because of their humble yet inspiring way of life.

So, I searched, and continue to search, for inspiration from them and the application of their mindsets, their extreme discipline, and their right habits in real life and workplace. The understanding of how we can be enemies to ourselves when it comes to fulfillment and achieving what we really desire in life prompted me to share and get it all out. Not only that, it was a true journey into myself that gave me clarity about what will come next.

In my book, Reimagine the Possible, I go into details of the attributes and tools of success and happiness, and how to apply them to your life. In this chapter, I am going to highlight some of them, to get you started on your road of possibilities.

THE WILL TO CHANGE

"It isn't the mountain ahead to climb that wears you down.

It's the pebbles in your shoes."
- Muhammad Ali

There are a few distinct features that set successful people apart from those who fail. It's not always the talent or number of titles they have behind their name, but it's their mindset and the few things they do differently than majority of us. First, they are able to develop strong and fulfilling relationships, alliances, and connections that will help them build their business, create their success, and open the doors to potential opportunities.

Second, they don't procrastinate, but act on their plan, and the things they passionately want to do. Often, what most people do is wait until the perfect time comes and put things off till tomorrow that they should do today; e.g. "I'll start my new online business when I get more support from my partner or the economy is better," or "I will create a better website for my business once my kids get out of the house." "I will start taking care of myself later." There is always a 'but' that we keep saying to ourselves.

Third, they don't give up, they are persistent, and they keep going with their plan. They understand that success will not be achieved instantaneously. How often do we start something but never finish it because it gets too tough, too time-consuming, or too overwhelming? If we face those few things and persevere, I believe, we might be quite successful and happy in our professional and personal lives.

Of course, the journey is never easy. Success doesn't happen overnight. It will take time, but if you believe in your abilities, have the right mindset and perseverance, and above all work hard, you will get there. The hard work is not only related to achieving your professional or career goals. It is also hard work on yourself, your beliefs, fears, and habits, all of which this chapter will discuss.

What's important is not what you will or will not do, or whether you will or will not change. It is whether you have the will to change – to plan and act so that you can start doing the things that you know you should.

NO SMOOTH MOUNTAIN

We keep dreaming about how one day we could reach our full potential, and the goals we always wanted to get to. But we often don't realize that we are as capable of genius as the most successful people in the world. We look at people like Oprah, Steve Jobs, and Richard Branson, and think, "If I only had their ideas, their genius", or "They are so lucky." You ask yourself, "How can I find my true purpose and passion in life? Why can't I never figure out how to be successful and happy like them?" But nobody, and especially the most successful in the world, thinks they are special until they make themselves special.

Nobody starts their business knowing that they will instantly become multi-billionaires. The difference starts with their mindset, the plan they have, and the actions they take. What sets the successful people apart from the less successful ones is that they do what most people don't want to do or are hesitant to do. Perhaps they hesitate because they are terrified of the unknown or they believe they are too busy, that it's beyond their capabilities, or maybe people around them would say it's not possible, that it is out of their reach and they will never get there. The other group, the fulfilled ones, listen to themselves and pursue their dreams, no matter the obstacles, and they ignore the naysayers.

Will you struggle? Will it be hard? Yes. You may fall many times, but who is counting? The best successes are made from failures. In fact, I don't believe there are failures, only lessons learned. You must remember that no single mountain is smooth. If you want to get to the top, there are sharp ridges that must be stepped over. There will be times that will be stressful, and you might be disappointed and discouraged.

FEAR

"No person can be confronted with a difficulty which has not the strength to meet and subdue. Every difficulty can be overcome if rightly dealt with. Anxiety is, therefore, unnecessary. The task which cannot be overcome ceases to be a difficulty and becomes impossibility and there's only one way of dealing with an impossibility, namely to submit to it."
- Byways of Blessedness, James Allen

When we are confronted with difficulties, over time they create a great amount of anxiety. We may be faced with decisions that have long-term ramifications for our life or career and would affect not only us, but also those close to us. Those are decisions that we would rather not have to make. They just make us want to pull a blanket over our head and wish they would disappear together with the light that disappears once the same blanket covers our hair.

The question that I started to ask myself was, "Where are my fears coming from and why am I allowing them to stop me from moving forward?

James Allen's words in the quote are very profound, and the essence is that there is no problem that cannot be resolved. I like to think about it in this way: if an issue that I am facing can be resolved with an action, then I don't have an issue. It is simply something that needs to be resolved and is just something that we encounter in our lives or at work. So, remember, if an issue can be solved with action, then it is not an issue.

This has been my approach to any challenge that has been placed in front of me throughout my career and life. I treat it like something exciting to resolve and put my best effort into coming up with the best solution.

A substantial body of research shows that our brain can't actually differentiate physical fear (e.g. car crash) from emotional fear (e.g. being afraid of a spider). In addition, research also shows that in the brain fear and excitement are caused by the same neurochemical signals, i.e. cortisol and norepinephrine. Steven Kotler talks about this at length in his research, and shows that fear and flow (or the peak performance) are at the opposite sides of the same spectrum. They are both caused by the same neurochemical reaction in the brain, initiated by cortisol and norepinephrine.

Successful people learn to reframe the fear and use it as their compass; if something that they want to do produces some level of fear, then this is exactly what they will do. They will do what scares them the most, what feels uncomfortable. Only by doing this will they be able to push their boundaries, and this will give them the progress and growth needed to accomplish what they want. Below are some ways that help to acknowledge and reframe fear:

1. Acknowledge the changes that are happening and how they are affecting you – how does the event make you feel?

2. Ask 'Do I have enough information and facts to support my fear?'

3. Reframe the context. Say to yourself that you are excited about the event. This will switch your brain from feeling anxious and nervous to feeling excited and positive (no danger is coming).

4. What's the payoff? What is the price that I will pay if I don't reframe and stay in the state of fear, which will negatively impact my performance and future prospects? What will my career look like?

You must remember that we fear and are anxious about things that we create in our minds and imagine that they may happen to us. We think that external forces create our anxiety or fear and we only respond to those events. But our response to any situation, however bad it may be, is our choice and the result of our thoughts and beliefs.

I always like to remind myself that most things that we imagine out of fear never happen. Mark Twain famously once said, "I have lived a long life and had many fears, most of which never happened."

MASTER THE MINDSET

"Beliefs have the power to create and power to destroy," as Tony Robbins, the motivational speaker and life coach, said. You see, our beliefs about the events around us or what happens to us are what shaped us into who we are today and who we will become tomorrow. But the fact is that many of us grew up around people who inadvertently passed on their limiting beliefs to us, and we might have been conditioned to the negative thinking that they grew up with. But remember, our past doesn't define us and there is no point in playing the blame game with them for passing their limiting beliefs onto you.

Research tells us that our thoughts and responses are shaped by our subconscious mind and they are aligned to the paradigms that we grew up with. For example, you might have had people in your life who constantly told you, "Since you haven't done it till now, you are just not cut out for it." This environment conditioned your thoughts and created paradigms in your subconscious mind. You start creating excuses without even realizing it, and eventually you will quit pursuing your dream.

If you want to have a successful career or follow your dreams, you need to evaluate whether your own mind is your biggest enemy and if you are acting according to old paradigms that shaped your thoughts, and hence your decisions, actions, and results. If so, a change is needed.

First, you will need to decide that you want to change your paradigm. Change is never easy, but once you realize that some of your old patterns, actions, and decisions are a result of the environment you were raised in or are surrounded by now, then you will see how this impacts your current life. I always like to remind myself of something that Wayne Dyer, American philosopher and author, said: "When you change the way you look at things, things that you look at change." Don't make yourself a victim of the circumstances surrounding you, or those that you cannot control.

Our life, career, and relationships are a reflection of the approach we take towards them. We are fully responsible for how things turn out for us – whether we are successful or not, have savings, a fulfilled relationship at home, a loving family, and so on. Let's say, your team is not producing the results you wish, or your business is not going well. Perhaps you are not paying attention to the relationships within your team and let them just run, or maybe the decisions you made were not the right ones. We are the only ones that have the power to take responsibility for the change we are looking for. We waste our most finite resource, time, to find external reasons that cause change. But once we shift this mindset, our life, career, and relationships will start getting into gear.

So, whatever we've learned and experienced in the past, we've accepted it as a truth at an unconscious level, and now it doesn't matter if what we've learned is correct or not, we still accept it as a truth. These are the 'life's apps' that we created for each aspect of our life – you have an app for everything that gives you a point of reference to go back to and check out how it should be done. I've realized over the years how this led to developing unconscious behaviors and habits in me.

"The beliefs that you have about yourself and your abilities are not facts. They are your tightly held opinions. In other words, it's not primarily about your ability. It's what you believe about your ability that shapes your potential success."
- Dr. Stan Beecham, Elite Minds

I also realized how often my belief system was empowering me or, unfortunately, disempowering me. You can take any experience in your life and make it into a very meaningful and empowering capability. Or it can be the opposite; your experiences and beliefs can be limiting you. You can take a painful experience and make it into powerful and motivating strength that will empower you to do anything you dreamt of.

There are a few simple ways that can help you work on your old paradigm and create change. I have done this myself, and it helped me realize how my own old conditioning was affecting my life, career, and relationships.

• Ask yourself: What are the same behaviors and actions that cause the same results and do not allow you to move forward?

- Think about successful people: What are the behaviors and actions they would take to get the results they want?

- Write down and focus on the new habits and actions that you want, and consciously think about them when you catch yourself doing the old ones.

- Change your 'I can't' or 'I should' to 'I must' and 'I will.'

DON'T DRIFT...DISCIPLINE

For any muscle on our body to grow, it needs to be exercised and maintained continuously. The same holds the true for everything we want to accomplish at work or in life. If you want to be accomplished in anything, you need to get disciplined in doing things that matter, that are important, to bring you closer to success and set you on the path to whatever you want to do in life.

Of course, there are times when we need to take a balanced approach, but discipline for me is really an intrinsic quality that we all should strive for. It comes from within and starts with you. Oftentimes, we are looking for all sorts of shortcuts – the new meditation technique that will set us free, the new set of motivational tools, and the new supplement to get our body fit. But these may (or may not) work for a week, a month or 3 months, and if it's not coming from within us, it won't last. We don't do hard things if we are not emotionally attached to them.

If you look at leaders you admire, or the most successful people, you will see the level of discipline they have in their lives, and in doing things that set them apart from others, things that others are not willing to commit to. It is an intrinsic self-discipline – a matter of 'personal will' as Jocko Willink, a retired navy SEAL officer, calls it. The difference between being good and being exceptional is how disciplined you are.

He continues by saying, "Those who are at work before everyone else are considered best operators." But that discipline cascades down to everything else they do. Willink rightly said, in his book Extreme Ownership, that discipline equals freedom. This is very true – once you are disciplined with the things that you know you should be doing, it sets you free to do other things that you claimed not having time for, but which were in fact just an excuse, with the blame pointed everywhere else but at yourself.

OWNERSHIP

One of the most important things I have learned, that really impacts how successful you will become, is to take full ownership of the results that you produce, the challenges, everything that impacts your results, or even your personal or social life. If I didn't own the results that were expected of me or my team to deliver, I would have never achieved the level and quality that I wanted. I always expect the highest results, but that can only be done if I completely own it. It is an attitude, and the fundamental block of any success. Blaming others or making excusing not only doesn't help but it actually hurts the team, the company, and ultimately you. In some cases, we don't want to even acknowledge the problem, or are afraid to accept that we made a mistake because we don't want to take ownership of the consequences. This will not serve the team or help it win.

Mistakes happen in the workplace, especially with complex problems, diverse teams, and tight deadlines. We should be able to acknowledge it, come up with better solutions for next time, or reach out to others for advice. We have much more respect for a person who takes full responsibility for their actions and results, don't we?

When we look at the great leaders and successful people around us, we wonder how they make the right decisions in stressful situations, or remain calm when faced with chaos and complexity. But what sets them apart in such situations is that they carefully choose how they respond. They don't jump to a conclusion and decide out of an emotional outbreak. This is a critical skill if you aspire to be a great leader and to be successful.

Often, what we do is react to situations without thinking, and we don't choose our behaviors but just act them out. We respond in the way our mind is wired and how we were conditioned. This may sometimes have catastrophic results in the workplace or in our personal lives.

Victor Frankl, the Austrian neurologist and psychiatrist, and a survivor of concentration camp, wrote a fascinating book "Man's Search for Meaning", in which he describes his horrific journey through Nazi concentration camps between 1942 and 1945, where he moved four times between different camps, including Auschwitz, while his family perished. Frankl said, "Between stimulus and response there is a space. In that space is our power to choose our response. In our response lies our growth and our freedom." This is a very profound thought that can guide us to make a shift in how we react and respond.

The best leaders and successful people train themselves and practice various scenarios for responding rather than reacting to the situation:

1. Think about consequences and bigger picture – What will you achieve by reacting in specific way (e.g. in anger)? Will the response

and consequences be aligned with your goals or plans? How will the response best serve you, your family, or your project and company?

2. Realize whether you are responding or reacting – This is important, because it will give you clarity if you are reacting out of anger, a lack of control, sadness, jealousy or perfectionism. If you pause and think about the root cause of your answer or reaction, you will be able to respond in a wiser, more thoughtful way.

3. Don't react out of emotions – This relates to the point above, but you will also need to realize that your best response is based on facts.

4. Realize that you have a choice and different options – When you are faced with a situation where you want to rush to react and respond harshly, realize that you have a choice, and consider the consequences of your reaction. Count to three, if you must.

HABITS

"What we know from lab studies is that it's never too late to break a habit. Habits are malleable throughout your entire life. But we also know that the best way to change a habit is to understand its structure — that once you tell people about the cue and the reward and you force them to recognize what those factors are in a behavior, it becomes much, much easier to change."
– Charles Duhigg 'Power of Habit'

A study was done by Wendy Wood, a Provost Professor of Psychology and Business at University of Southern California, on a group of people that was given stale popcorn in the cinema in exchange for rating a move. Most of the people ate the stale popcorn despite the fact that they said after the movie that they didn't like it. It turned out that they ate it out of their habit of being in the cinema. But what this shows us is that we often do things without realizing it and a, "Thoughtful intentional mind is easily derailed, and people tend to fall back on habitual behaviors," said Wood.

From the time you get up in the morning until you go to bed – most of what you do in between is without thinking; it's automatic. I mention automatic because it is a very important feature of habits, because we don't even realize what we are doing and why we do it. In fact, 40% to 45% of our daily activities is habitual, according to Professor Wood.

Everything we do or want to do is a step towards accomplishing a goal or achieving something that we desire – that goal might be to get to work, to satisfy hunger, to relax, to feel wanted, to get a promotion, and so on. Professor Wood explains that, "We find patterns of behavior that allow us to reach our goals. We repeat what works, and when actions are repeated in a stable context, we form associations between cues and responses."

It turns out that our brain creates patterns of activities, thinking, and behaviors that we do constantly and become automatic, so it doesn't have to spend energy to think about it each time (a simple example would be how to walk or brush your teeth). Our brain developed habits, so it doesn't have to think about them repeatedly and can have the space to focus on doing what's more important, like new projects at work, creating new product, writing, studying, making decisions, and more.

When we behave out of habit, our mental activity and alertness drops in the middle of it. Research shows that once we develop a habit and do something on autopilot, our brain is almost inactive, and so is our decision capability related to that activity. For example, when you are driving to work, you don't think, "Ok, now I need to decide to indicate that I want to turn right," do you? You don't make these decisions any more. When you were driving to work for the first time, you perhaps needed to think about which street to turn right onto. Over time, it became automatic.

Habits are developed slowly, and it is very hard for us to change the habit without completely knowing what the cues of that habit are. We must learn how to identify which cues led to a particular behavior, called cue awareness, so that we are at least aware and know when the habit is actually happening. Oftentimes, with certain strong behaviors, we don't realize the cue and, hence, we do them automatically. For example, some people bite their nails without realizing it, and they may now understand what the cue is (i.e. why they are doing it).

Have you found yourself with any habit that you do without understanding why, and you only realize it once you've done it? The important part of a change is to do it slowly through first recognizing when we have the urge or need to do the habit.

All successful people understand the importance of small improvements, which underpin our progress and have a profound impact on the long-term improvement. Imagine if you made just one tiny improvement every day. That small change, done every day, will turn into a habit and it will become part of your subconscious.

In the Japanese culture, this is called kaizen, which literally means 'improvement' or 'change for better,' and is fundamental to their professional lives and personal relationships. But the Japanese also understand that to see the change, we need to commit to it. Very often, what happens is that we set a goal, such as something that we want to improve. We might get excited and motivated at first, but that commitment fades after a few weeks and we forget to keep up our commitment. This comes back to understanding the triggers and wanting to change.

The single most important thing is our full commitment and then acting upon it. Without it, we will return to your original state in days. We really must be disciplined. At the end of the day, the most successful athletes didn't achieve their gold medals without true discipline. Yes, we will have obstacles, bad days, and days where we just can't do it anymore, but remember, after winter comes spring and summer. Don't think your winter will last forever.

Start small. Don't overwhelm yourself with too many things that you think you should, or want to, improve. It will only confuse you and you won't be able to achieve anything. To change your behavior long-term, you will need to:

1. increase your performance little by little every day, and

2. change your environment to get rid of the distractions that may keep you close to your old habits and behavior.

"We are what we repeatedly do.
Excellence, then, is not an act, but a habit."
- Aristotle

GROWTH AND FAILURE

There are no happy accidents that turn people into experts or that give people some special gift which allows them to live a happy and successful life. We are not born into it. While some could be genetic, most of it is not. When we are born, our potential is unknown. We can accomplish whatever we can possibly imagine, and our abilities can be developed.

When we read about successful people or observe those around us who seem to have more success than us, be it better jobs, better relationships, or better health, what they all actually have in common is their constant hunger for growth and development. They never stop learning new things and upskilling themselves, their mind is always curious, and they want to push the boundaries of what is possible. All these characteristics underpin their growth mindset, which is critical to their progression.

"When you are in a fixed mindset, your success is a result of that belief. And all you will try to do throughout your life is to prove yourself against that fixed standard. In a growth mindset, challenges are exciting rather than threatening. So, rather than thinking, "Oh, I'm going to reveal my weaknesses," you say, "Wow, here is a chance to grow."
- Dr. Carol Dweck

Growth mindset is a scientific theory suggesting that with effort, persistence, and hard work, our intelligence and abilities can be developed. Dr. Carol Dweck, a psychology professor for Stanford University, showed through over twenty years of study of human development and psychology that our belief system about our abilities and potential fuel our behavior and predict our success. Dr. Dweck's early research was focused on how kids respond to failure, and shows how some children reacted positively to failures and setbacks, taking them as opportunities to develop, while others were completely devastated by them. Those kids who thrived on challenges adopted a growth mindset. They believed that with hard work, good strategies, and perseverance, they would eventually develop more skills and talents. Those who wanted to stay away from failure at all costs were in the fixed mindset.

"It's not how good you are. It's how good you want to be."
- Paul Arden

Very often, we see people who have very fixed beliefs about their abilities, what can be done or achieved, and what they can accomplish in their career or in life. For example, you hear at work, "This cannot be possibly done," or "It's beyond my capabilities." Perhaps we may see that in ourselves at times. We may think, "I'm not good at this," instead of "What am I missing?"; "This is too hard," instead of "This may take some time and effort,"; or "I'm obviously not good at finance," instead of "I'm not good at finance yet and keep studying."

People who don't progress through their lives or career only see obstacles that prevent them from achieving what they want, or what is achievable at all. They look at their abilities, skills, and performance, or even their health, fitness, and relationships as fixed and accept them as they are. This "fixed mindset," as Dr. Dweck describes, "makes us believe that our character, intelligence, and creative ability are static and cannot change or improve in any meaningful way."

You may see multiple examples of a fixed mindset around you. There might have been several projects or initiatives that were believed to not be achievable or were too hard to implement, and hence were abandoned. A project manager believed that the timeline was too short; there were no right skills or resources within the team; no right leadership or systems to support it; and the reasons why not could go on forever. Focusing on issues rather than solutions, and the things that would prevent the team from being successful would, indeed, bring no results.

With the right mindset and approach, even hard tasks can be achieved, issues can be resolved, and step by step, you will take the team closer to success. Remember that if an issue can be resolved with actionable tasks, you actually don't have an issue. This requires the right mindset to be in place, one that will see unlimited potential and the bending of the boundaries of what's possible.

This is what successful people do. If we look at the people whose success we admire, then we will see that they cultivate their growth mindset to enable their personal, professional, and social development and progression. Research shows that one of the reasons why we feel unhappy or frustrated in our jobs or personal lives is that we stop growing and progressing. We, as humans, are "designed" to evolve, and progress and growth is necessary to our wellbeing.

"If you imagine less, you will be what you undoubtedly deserve."
- Debbie Millman

With the growth mindset, as Dr. Dweck explains, we treat any setback as an integral part of our development and path to success. I have felt bad, embarrassed, or fearful of my mistakes and setbacks, but I've learnt that they would only help me to grow. Often, I came out on the short end with my decisions, but every time I aimed to tweak my approach to do better next time.

Growth mindset keeps our mind sharp. In today's work environment, we need to keep up with new technological and organizational developments. Things are changing and won't slow down anytime soon. To be ahead, we need to constantly learn.

Sometimes we find ourselves in moments where our fixed mindset kicks in, but the important thing is to realize it, snap out of that, consider more appropriate approach and move forward. Through "deliberate practice" we can change it – we must be purposeful and systematic about what we want to change. What helps me shift when I find myself in a fixed state are the four simple steps outlined below. They require a focused attention, and once you go through them, you will realize how destroying and limiting your fixed mindset can be, and instead will focus on developing more of a growth one.

1. Be aware that you are exposed to limiting thoughts based on your past and learn to be aware of your fixed mindset thoughts. What I mean by that is that we are prone to reject new opportunities, not because we are not able to do it, but because we are afraid of the unknown. Our brain is wired to search past experiences and do only what is known and in our comfort zone. Remember that this is only your brain's response to the unknown. It wants to keep you safe and it doesn't like risks and any unpredictability.

2. Acknowledge that you have the choice. We all have a choice about how we react and respond to any situation. How you interpret challenges, setbacks, and criticism is your choice. Whether you apply a fixed or growth mindset, it will have a chain reaction in what will happen next.

3. Replace fixed mindset talk with a growth mindset voice. Personally, I have had many moments when I dealt with self-doubt and feared to take on new challenging projects, was simply procrastinating, or too lazy to do something. We have all been there. Over the years, though,

I have learned to replace those damaging thoughts of a fixed mindset with the empowering thoughts and beliefs for growth. When I doubted myself and thought, "Can I do this? This is certainly not for me. I don't have the talent to do this," I immediately replaced those thoughts with empowering thoughts, such as, "I am certain I can do this and I will learn along the way," "I have passion and perseverance to accomplish this."

4. Take action that focuses on growth. Without action, there is no progress. Without facing the challenges and new opportunities, you will never learn. You must wholeheartedly commit to the challenge and overcoming any setbacks that will come your way. Learn from it and adjust as necessary.

FAILURES ARE YOUR GIFT

It is no secret that our worst fear is a fear of failure. However, failure is actually a good thing. It is just an opportunity to begin again, learn from it, and to do it more wisely next time. Encouraging our fears and failures prompts the most necessary changes in our lives and businesses. This may be true, but we don't often feel or think like that.

When we make mistakes, we feel terrible and disappointed; we lose confidence, and get discouraged. We just don't want to continue or go through it again. What we are actually doing is missing out on the primary benefit of failure. Winston Churchill once said, "Success is the ability to go from one failure to another without losing your enthusiasm." The man was right.

When it comes to failures, our egos are our own worst enemies. When something is going wrong, we try to save face and our defence mechanisms kick in, and we often find ourselves in denial. It seems very hard for us to admit and to try to learn from failure, because it requires us to challenge our status quo.

"I haven't failed. I have just found 10,000 ways that won't work."
- Thomas Edison

Look at Walt Disney, who was fired from the local newspaper he worked for because he was told he had no imagination. What his story teaches us is that just because you encounter a setback or end up on another path, it doesn't mean that you are stuck. Keep learning from your mistakes, apply changes to make things better, and you will get back on track eventually, and most likely, you will be better off than before.

There are many successful people who we can mention here who have failed but never gave up, e.g. Steve Jobs, Oprah, JK Rowling. What separates successful people from those who are unsuccessful is that they have a huge amount of perseverance. They never give up or let their failures define them. They pick themselves up even stronger than before and keep going. It's not always easy to continue moving forward, but when you keep pushing onwards, despite the failures and obstacles along the way, you are already ahead of all those people that just gave up. I find that the secret really is to just show up and try your best over and over again.

Failures are part of the process. To be successful, you must learn how to make it a tool rather than a roadblock. You must be adaptable and agile. When you stop learning from your mistakes, then you will stop growing and developing. You should take any failure as motivation in pursuit of your dreams. Don't let it stop you but grow you instead. The only failure there can be is when you quit. Learn the lessons, apply them, and you will come out stronger than before. You will never learn faster than you will by executing something.

NOTHING HAPPENS WITHOUT ACTION

Remember, talk is cheap! Action is everything. Our thoughts are catalysts to get started. But our thoughts are not things, and nothing will happen without taking those thoughts and putting them into action mode. That's what successful people focus on. They know that talking, planning, and analysing won't get them too far. It's their actions that will trigger all the things on their road to success. To be successful in any part of your life, you must be action-oriented. Mark Twain said, "The secret to getting ahead is getting started." You can't do everything at once, but you can take it step by step. Incremental changes every day will work in the long run.

Try to keep the momentum to get you closer to where you want to be. You can develop a plan to work on your habits and then pick one to focus on at the time. Commit to it!

BANNISTER EFFECT

One of my favourite stories, which I would like to finish off with and which I personally find very inspiring, is the story called The Bannister Effect. In moments of doubt or thinking that something is not possible, I always return to it and remind myself that what I might believe is not possible can actually be achieved. Before 1954, it was believed that running one mile under 4 minutes was physically impossible, that the human body could not possibly do it. In 1954, Roger Bannister, an English middle-distance athlete, ran it in 3.59 minutes, breaking what was believed to be an impossible record. But what happened next is remarkable – once it was known that the mile could be run in under 4 minutes, many other athletes accomplished it, and with even better results.

What this shows us is that it was not a sudden leap in the evolution of the human body that broke the physical barriers. It was a shift in thinking. Bannister truly believed that it was possible to run faster and break the record. He visualised himself achieving it over and over, and his mind accepted it as reality. The story also shows us that once we see that something can be done, something that was once believed to be outside of our realm of possibilities, we can also achieve it.

In our daily work or life, our mindset has the ability to limit us or set us up to achieve the impossible, not only for us but those around us, our team, our peers, and our family. We are in control of whether we will conform to what is socially accepted or try to believe beyond it. If Bannister believed that the record was 4 minutes, and nothing could be done about it, that it was a physical limitation, then he would never have been able to break it. He would never even have tried to do it.

Just like this story, what often keeps us from achieving what we truly want is the barriers that only exist in our mind.

To connect with Anna Griffin please visit
www.ReimagineThePossible.com

The Yellow Lights in Life Matter, Reset and Go

JIM HETHERINGTON

*"If we did all the things we are capable of,
we would literally astound ourselves."*

– Thomas Edison

I stood staring into the eyes of a 700-pound tiger, hoping I would survive the encounter.

In my early 20s I had the privilege of working for the African Lion Safari in Ontario, Canada for five years. It was a thrill for me. I loved the animals and being outside. I guess I was good at what I did because in my second summer season there the manager walked up to the supervisor and myself and said, "Steve you're out. Jim you're in."

In other words, Steve was demoted and I was promoted. The manager of the park didn't like the way the supervisor was running his section.

There was no training and I had no experience. All of a sudden, I was responsible for lions, tigers, cheetahs, and bears. Oh my.

The next summer, my boss came up to me and said, "On my days off I want you to take my responsibilities."

He did not like doing radio interviews, TV interviews, or getting animals ready to be transported to another zoo. So, along with the responsibility of supervising a dozen or more staff, and overseeing about 1,000 animals on 800 acres of park, I covered for him on his days off. And guess what things were scheduled when my boss took his days off? You guessed it, interviews and the occasional animal that needed to be transported.

That's where the tiger comes in. Remember, I did not receive any real training; I learned as I went.

"We don't have enough time to get anymore help, we have to get this animal shifted," I yelled to one of my co-workers as we looked at this 700-pound tiger. It was sedated, laying on the ground in front of us as we tried to lift it from the ground and slide it into a transport cage.

Half an hour earlier, the staff and I were standing in front of the tiger's cage evaluating the situation. We had a 700-pound Siberian male tiger that needed to be transported to another park. So, it was my responsibility to come up with a plan, figure out how I was going to transport it, sedate it, and execute the plan — without any troubles or casualties.

I made the plan, got my staff together, and prepared the transport cage, which was on a trailer and raised about 6 inches off the ground. We had to back it up as close as we could to the pen, dart the animal, and, with our hands and ropes, slide it into the cage so that we could transport it. Seemed like an easy task.

I headed up to the office and unlocked the locker with the sedation medication and the dart gun. After I figured how much the animal weighed, I proceeded to calculate how much sedative I needed. I made the dart, grabbed the gun, hopped in my truck, and went back out to the park.

We stood in front of the cage and I waited for the ideal shot. I got a clean shot right in the back leg and we just stood and waited for the animal to fall asleep.

After about ten minutes we noticed that the animal was just sitting there staring at us. He was dopey and kind of grumbling a little bit. He was wavering back and forth, but he wasn't sleeping. It was then that I recalculated the amount of medication I sedated him with and realized that I underestimated his weight by about 250 pounds.

I raced back up to the office, got more medication, made another dart, came out and stood in front of the pen. I made another shot to almost the exact same spot. Then, we waited.

Five minutes later, the animal was flat, completely asleep. So we opened up the door and began to execute our simple plan.

Sliding him across even ground wasn't so bad. It was that 6-inch hump up into the transport cage that was the problem. I held his head and neck to keep him safe and to guide his shoulders up. What a struggle.

71

We repositioned ourselves so many different times, but still we could barely budge him up there. His shoulders were on the top of the cage, but we still had the rest of the body to come up with him. We just could not move him. One of the staff suggested he goes and gets more people to help. This started a bit of a debate.

As we were discussing, all of a sudden my hands turned and the cat was now staring into my eyes! Two things I noticed here. One the eyes were dilated which could have been from the drugs. The second thing I noticed was the eyes were green and I knew that was reserved for when Tigers get frightened or angry. Either way, I wasn't comfortable looking into these eyes. His mouth opened and he began to grumble and growl. At this moment I wasn't any happier than he was about our position.

I looked at the men who were around and yelled, "We don't have time to get anymore help, we have to get this animal shifted."

Within two minutes, we had that animal up – adrenaline kicked in and we slid him into the cage. We had no sooner got his back legs in, his tail in and closed the door, that he was sitting up inside this cage looking at us.

It's amazing what you can do when a tiger is waking up and you have no more time left. All of a sudden, what was impossible before became possible.

YELLOW LIGHTS ARE IMPORTANT

Many times in life, we run into situations that we are not sure how to deal with. When this happens, we may formulate a plan as we go with the hopes that things will work out. It's like driving along when all the traffic lights are green and then coming up on one that turns yellow. Then we have a decision to make: are we going to speed up and try to race through it, lock on the brakes, or just casually slow down and come to a stop?

Often, it's the same in our personal lives, our work lives, and our spiritual lives. A lot of us have that same approach when we encounter an unexpected situation that we are not sure of. We treat it like that yellow light. We could rush through without thinking about the consequences, we could jam on the brakes and stop everything because we can't handle it, or we could slow down and take the time to assess the situation.

Yellow lights are important in our lives. If we are in a situation, let's say in a business meeting that didn't go that well, the yellow light is the areas where we could have changed or done better. We evaluate the delivery. We evaluate what we said. We rethink how we approached the meeting or situation.

The problem is, sometimes when we get into those situations, we try to push our way through, like speeding up to get through the yellow light before it changes. We don't want to stop, we don't want to take the time to evaluate what happened. Often, we don't realize that maybe we were wrong or that there were things we needed to change.

The yellow light is the time to slow down and think about that meeting, think about that proposal, think about that relationship and how we interacted with that person. Look for ways we can adjust our thinking or adjust how we could have done it better. We need to look at the whole thing and be honest with ourselves. The yellow stands for "yell out." We need to speak out the frustration or tension we feel, and be open to adjust our thinking and our mindset.

The red light stands for "redo." We need to redo our thinking. When we reset our mindset and re-shift ourselves, we can decide how we will approach the situation if it happens again.

Red lights are a great time to reposition our hearts and redirect our attitudes. Red lights aren't always an inconvenience. They can be good for us too. By taking the time to really look at our heart and attitude, we can then move forward in a more positive manner.

Most of us have been frustrated with something or someone in the past. Imagine a time you were so frustrated you felt like spitting, and steam was coming out of your nostrils. Rather than giving in, you persistently pressed on, trying to win the argument or get your point across. You kept at the task with all the determination in the world, trying to overcome the obstacle. Finally, after a trying time, imagine you stopped and took a break. You got some fresh air, took a little walk, counted to ten, and took deep breaths.

To your amazement, as you went back to the situation it's like a cloud has lifted. All of a sudden, you were communicating, and it was actually working. You tried the task again and all the parts fit and worked as planned.

Was it a miracle? No. That's the result of slowing down (yellow light) and then stopping (red light) and seeing things in a new light.

Which leads us to the next step.

The green light. The green light is when you get going and decide that you are going to use that new mindset. The green light is you moving forward and doing things differently. This is where you apply what you have learned during the yellow and red lights.

It's the same in the relationships in your life. You can ignore what is going on or you can reflect and allow the relationship to become stronger. Let me give you a practical example.

How many times have you gotten into this situation? It's 7 o'clock in the morning, you got up late, and you are rushing to get everybody ready to go off to school and work. There are tensions and frustrations. You are getting under each other's feet. You part ways and everyone, including you, is in a sour mood. By the time you get to work, you are disheartened and ready to throw in the towel; you'd rather go back home to bed. Then, you go through the day thinking about it. You go over in your mind what went wrong, how it went wrong, and the awful things that were said.

The yellow light could be where you say to yourself, "How can I take a different approach to the way I spoke to my spouse, my children, or my significant other? How can I realign myself and speak out in a different way?"

The red light is realizing that you can't control that other person. You can't always control your work scenario or your home scenario, but you can control yourself and the way that you react.

I can control the way I speak out. I control my attitude. I don't have to allow my children or spouse to change my attitude. I can take responsibility for that and keep myself in check. The green light is to go and work on implementing the ideas you came up with.

YOUR SPIRITUAL LIFE

Sometimes in our spiritual life we can get frustrated with the universe, the world, and God because we don't think they are delivering what we desire. We don't think we are getting what we want.

That yellow light is recognizing that something is not right inside you or around you. That may be why you feel like you're being ripped off or not getting the answers that you want. Many times, those emotions are deep down. Instead of seeing the emotions, you see their effects.

The red light is to sit and realign yourself with your core values, core beliefs, and to see that God and the universe can be trusted. Maybe it is your beliefs that need to be strengthened. Ask for guidance. It will come in time. This is where belief comes in. Put action to your mindset and see it become reality.

THE CONSEQUENCES OF CONSTANTLY RUNNING THROUGH THE YELLOW LIGHT

One of the dangers of racing through the yellow light and ignoring that warning is that by the time you get through the intersection that light could be red. Now you are not going through a caution warning, you are going through a red light and there could be consequences.

From the driving side of things, you know what that is. If there is a police officer nearby, they could be hot on your tail and pull you over to give you a traffic violation. That could mean points and it could be dollars. It could be a lot of things. If you require that license for business, for travelling, or for making your income, you can only lose so many points before you are going to start getting into trouble.

From the life side of things, you may be ignoring warning signs. If you ignore these caution signs and yellow lights you are going to have to face the consequences.

One consequence in your business life could be continuing to not make sales. If you are unwilling to adjust your attitude or approach, then the consequence might be that you never get customers.

In relationships, if you keep plowing through thinking that there is nothing wrong and that yellow light is for someone else, the consequence might be a very unhappy, unfulfilled relationship. The frustrating and confrontational situations may never go away or get resolved.

If you think that everybody else is the problem, then you are never going to grow, or have a healthy and happy relationship. We need to take time, slow down, then stop completely and re-evaluate our approach to relationships before proceeding with a new attitude.

One of the dangers in life is we stop reading. They say the average person reads maybe two books through the rest of their life after high school, college, or university.

You get into the habit of just doing your job or going through your routines. If you don't adjust, the danger is you become stunted and don't grow and mature as a person.

Psychology teaches that by the time we are 35 years old 90 percent of thinking is just habitual. So if we don't interrupt that by continuing to build new habits and re-evaluate old ones (this could be replacing or re-surrounding old habits with new habits) we are in danger of staying the same person all the way through into our later stages of life.

About ten years ago, I had to step back and evaluate my life. I was at a time where I was working far too hard through the day. I was doing projects in the evening and working steady for seven days a week. Eventually, it caught up to me. I became depressed and tired and burnt out. It took me a long time to get myself back up there.

That period of time allowed me to reflect on what I was doing, how I was doing it, and how it was working for me. Quite honestly, my lifestyle wasn't working for me very well. That's what caused the burn-out. I had to acknowledge that I was striving for success and not getting there. I burned myself out in the process.

During that time of burn-out I was physically, mentally, and emotionally drained. I couldn't function. I was self-employed at the time, and I had customers that I had to serve and take care of. But I found that I was only able to work one or two days a week.

It took me a long time to get back up and I sacrificed a lot of income through that time because I had to surrender the contracts I couldn't fulfill. For me, it was a huge consequence that, because I had burned out, I couldn't fulfill the jobs that I already had.

Relationally, it was also very challenging. I have a very forgiving and very gracious wife and she was very patient with me at the time. I went through a period of six months where I said minimal words because I just didn't have the mental capacity or strength to verbalize my thoughts and emotions. It was too draining even to try.

THE TIME IS NOW

You need to step back and evaluate your life, daily, weekly, monthly, and yearly. You can only grow when you see what you must change. It is not other people's responsibility to change to what you want. You need to become more. You need to evaluate you.

Those yellow lights are the perfect time to slow down, pause, prepare to stop at the red lights, and take a reality check. What areas of your life need adjustment? What areas can you improve in? Remember that what you do affects everyone else, so by changing yourself for the better, others see it and it encourages them to do the same.

Don't look at red lights as an inconvenience anymore. If you need to stop at one STOP! Take the time to be grateful. Take the time to think about things in your life that you could change. Think of past encounters or meetings and think on how you might handle them differently next time. Don't rush through. Stop and reflect.

My tiger story at the beginning of the chapter? It is there to show that nothing is impossible. You may feel overwhelmed right now or at the edge of burnout. When you hit those times of life, it feels like life is impossible and that nothing will ever change. That is the way I felt, but I made it through. When things are at their worst, heed the yellow light and slow down to evaluate. If you keep speeding through, you will be stopped, whether it is by a police officer or by the other car that is trying to get through that same yellow light.

So, make the choice to slow down and stop. Don't plow through life trying to avoid every red light. As the old expression goes, 'life is a journey, not a destination'. Pause, stop, and proceed only after you have reflected, re-adjusted, and re-aligned yourself.

Would you like more resources? These extra resources will help you realize the relationships you want and to find the balance necessary to succeed. Go to www.YourRelationshipRescueCoach.com to check out other resources and articles that are available for you. Also, be sure to go to www.IncreaseTheLove.com to find other books that are available for you.

I would love an opportunity to sit down with you and discuss your unique situation. So please reach out to me at jim@yourrelationshiprescuecoach.com and let's book a complimentary consultation. During our 30 minutes, either in person or on Zoom, you and I will discuss areas that may be sabotaging your relationships, together we will create a crystal-clear vision, discuss a plan moving forward and send you on your way refreshed and re-energized.

During our session we can discuss ways to create an environment that better suits your needs and talk about ways to keep the momentum going forward. You and I will discuss ways that you can avoid colliding at life's intersection and discover how to apply principles that will help you navigate a healthy and balanced course.

Remember, it's not about how quickly you can blast through your day or your meetings, but it's about the quality interactions that you have along the way. If you will take moments to pause and reflect you may just find the days, weeks, months and years go smoother and more enjoyable over time.

To a life of enjoying the red lights,
Jim Hetherington

You Set Your Own Appraisal

DR. SOBIA YAQUB

In its early years, plastic surgery was a miracle, a way to correct everything that you might have seen as an imperfection in your appearance. Yet, a funny thing began to manifest as plastic surgery became more widely available. People were never satisfied. For every fix, they saw another imperfection that needed to be corrected. Beautiful individuals were putting themselves under the knife, because they wanted to attain a level of perfection that was impossible.

What was the problem? Surprisingly enough, it had nothing to do with their physical bodies at all. It was their viewpoint and perspective. It was because they were giving all their power to other people and putting more value in other people's perception and opinion than their own opinion of themselves.

They were so focused on their outside that they ignored the issues and lack of confidence they had about who they were as individuals. They ignored the internal dialogue that kept manifesting in feelings of not being good enough, not being beautiful enough, and simply just not being enough.

"Whatever the mind can conceive and believe, the mind can achieve."
– Napoleon Hill

If you struggle in this area, I want you to understand that you can make a change. It starts with recognizing that your outside is a reflection of what you are focusing on inside. Once you change how you speak to yourself, then you will be able to accept and love yourself inside and out. I mean you have to redefine your self-image, which is independent of the opinions of others. That means getting to know your authentic self, not what was or is expected of you by others but what you truly, deep down from the bottom of your heart, expect from yourself. You do this by eliminating all kinds of fear, including fear of rejection, fear of disapproval, and fear of humiliation. If we look at history, the people who received the most approval from the world were the ones who were crystal clear about who they were and what they stood for, completely independent of others' opinions or perceptions about them. You can never reach your full potential unless you have healthy self-esteem.

I want you to imagine yourself in your car in New York City and amidst heavy traffic, trying to reach your desired destination by following your GPS. It is supposed to take you to the desired location, but keeps redirecting you again and again, taking you back home. It is extremely frustrating. Can you imagine saying to yourself: "Why is this GPS taking me home, which is far away from where I want to go?" It's because when you started your journey, you accidently selected home as your destination.

Similarly, when we were little, long before we started navigating our journey in this life, we formed a concept of ourselves, our abilities and expectations from ourselves and the world, which is called self-esteem or self-image. It is formed through our childhood experiences and our interpretation of those experiences, mainly with the authority figures in our lives, and somewhat by our peers and other people we interact with.

This concept of "self-esteem" serves as the destination of GPS. I believe by the time we are 7 years old, we have an almost complete concept of how the world is, who we are, and what space we occupy in relation to the world and the people around us. All our life, we behave and make decisions based upon that concept, unless it is fine-tuned by any significant life-altering event. Now imagine if that self-image was faulty and wrong as it was formed mainly through the years when we did not have a conscious or logical mind, and it was under control of the circumstances and people around us.

This means that our self-image and self-esteem, which is shaping our destiny each moment by the way we think, feel, act and react, depends on the intellect of the people around us as we were growing up, based on their limited perception about us as a child. Can you imagine that the most important factor which governs literally everything in our life has been formed without our informed consent?

This self-esteem or self-image was formed when we did not have insight about our true worth and is based on what we believed about ourselves as a child. If we were unfortunate enough to develop low self-esteem, then unless we fix our faulty self-esteem by reinterpreting the past experiences and making new sense of ourselves and the world, we cannot reach our goals and desires that are not congruent with our self-esteem.

IT STARTS WITH RECOGNIZING YOUR OWN VALUE

Self-image or self-esteem is defined as one's concept of oneself or of one's role and worth in this world. When you take the power back to redefine yourself and your true worth, you are putting yourself in the driver's seat to have the life that you deserve.

We all deserve to have wonderful things happen, to enjoy amazing experiences, to raise our families with values and beliefs that we cherish, and to find peace as we grow and learn throughout our journeys. Too often, however, we end up tripping ourselves up, because we focus on what we don't have, what isn't working, and allow our grief about what we have lost to keep us from seeing all that we have gained.

A key filtering system in our brain, which acts in congruence with our self-esteem and goals, is the Reticular Activating System (RAS). It serves as our slave. It is a network of neurons, which are located in the brain stem. It filters billions of bits of data and information, filters in the information that is important for us or that can serve us based on its alignment with our self-esteem. Have you ever noticed that when you decide you want to buy a car, say a Honda Accord, that you start seeing them everywhere?

It is as if, in the moment you decide on that vehicle, your RAS is activated. All of a sudden, Honda Accords, which were not within your awareness before, suddenly come into your awareness. In fact, you can count on your fingers how many Honda Accords passed you on the road that day.

Similarly, when you have a certain level of self-esteem or a certain self-image impressed upon your mind, your RAS will filter in the people, conditions, and opportunities that will help you achieve a life or goals congruent with your self-image. There is a term in the field of psychology named "Cognitive Dissonance," which is an uncomfortable state of mind when there are two or more inconsistent thoughts and beliefs. When you create a higher self-image, you create that dissonance between your old ways of being, thinking, feeling, communicating, and other habits that are not in sync with the new image. Your mind will then reject your old ways, thus propelling you to act in accordance with your new elevated self-esteem and self-image.

Throughout this chapter, I am focusing on how you can achieve a better life for yourself by creating a different mental picture of yourself. No matter who you are, you have a mental picture of yourself. Society also has an impact on molding your self-image. There are those expectations that you feel compelled to meet, and there is a guilt that seems to be built into all of us when we don't achieve those expectations.

Going through my own battle with low self-esteem, and after helping thousands of people conquer their low self-esteem, now your battle is my battle, as I know exactly who our enemy is and how we can kill that enemy. In other words, I can find out quite easily whether you have low self-esteem, which is holding you back from achieving your goals and dreams in any area of your life, what factors caused your faulty self-esteem, and how to fix it. Low self-esteem can be the root cause of obesity, failure in shedding those extra pounds, disturbed relationships, broken marriages, domestic violence, poor grades in school, issues with lack of money, failure in business, fear of speaking, social anxiety, compliance with medications, and in literally any area of life where you are struggling. I bet there is low self-esteem hiding there in your mind's GPS as your set destination, causing you to fail and come back to the same place over and over again.

Amidst all these factors, it can be easy to focus on the negative when it comes to your self-image and self-worth. It can be easy to look for quick fixes, instead of looking at the reasons why you feel a certain way about yourself. Fixing the outside is not going to fix the inside. Instead, you have to decide what you deserve and then focus on achieving that.

I was blessed to be born and raised in an amazing family with really high academic standards and a strong discipline. My mother and father are the most supportive parents I have seen, who invested so much time and energy to make us independent and successful human beings. We had servants, chefs and a chauffeur at our disposal all the time. All we were expected to do was to study and get good grades. My father served in the military as a commando. He was passionate about his duty. He fought in two wars. He was the best athlete of his time in the army, and he participated and represented our country in the world's military championship in Athens, Greece. He attributes this to his unshakeable belief in himself and his abilities, and of course the help of God.

My mom is an amazing lady. She is the most hard-working woman I have ever seen, with extraordinary resolve and perseverance. She had very high expectations for her children's education, and a vision for our performance in the world, and she was and still is very much involved in our lives. With an academically challenging environment at home, my oldest brother grew up to be a civil engineer and the rest of us, four siblings, became medical doctors. As the youngest, I was treated as the "baby of the house." I was pampered, spoon-fed, and guided in every step. My siblings were all exceptionally good in studies, and particularly in science and math, which were not my strengths. I was an artist and I had a passion for fine arts. Literally all my school books were full of pictures of faces and cartoons that I drew.

I used to represent my school in fine arts competitions, but somehow, I developed low self-esteem because I was constantly gauging myself based upon understanding of concepts of math and science. I overlooked my strengths. I was comparing my weaknesses with my siblings' strengths.

My friends in childhood were a reflection of my low self-esteem, as I made friends with the kids who were the "back benchers." I was associating myself with the low achievers. My group of friends and I were the ones who would never listen to the lectures and made fun of the teachers. To the utter surprise of others, I would get really good results at the end of the year because I learnt some techniques to accelerate my comprehension and retention. My focus would be as sharp as a laser and I would lock myself in a room with a set of goals and deadlines that I resolved to achieve, in order to keep up with my siblings. Of course, my friends used to get jealous of me because they believed I did not deserve to get better grades than them.

I was a shy kid, but I was genuinely interested in people and always wanted to help them. That was a reason I bought into my mother's vision of me becoming a doctor.

While my older brothers and sisters managed to have a huge library with books in alphabetical order on the shelves, I would seldom read a single book. Still, I managed to write my own book of poems, and create my little magazines every few months with pictures cut from different magazines, containing my own observations about different actors and TV programs. I started all that when I was 8 years old. Our friends, and guests to our home, were amused to see my funny magazines and my poems. My sister used to tell me I was very observant and creative. I spent most of my day in my room with my dolls, painting or writing, because I was not comfortable among people as I was shy.

The education system in Pakistan is very different from the American system. We have two major exams. The first is at the end of 10th grade, which determines whether you will go into Pre-Med, and one at 12th grade, which determines whether you will get admission in the medical school.

Some moments in your life can make a drastic change in the course of your life. I remember that one day of my school vividly. I was in 10th grade and it was the last quarter of the year. I was, as usual, sitting in the very back row with my "not so motivated" friends, not paying attention to the teacher and drawing my friend's face on my book. Our math teacher, who was no less than terror for the class, caught me. She knew my whole family and had taught my two older sisters. She called me to the front and asked me to solve the problem on the blackboard. I had no clue at first, since I had not been listening and, second, math was never my strength. I could not solve the problem. She gave me a stern look and in front of the whole class said, "Sobia, this was such a simple problem and you failed to solve it. The board exams are around the corner. All of your brothers and sisters excelled in studies and I am certain that won't be able to keep up with the image of your family and you can never become a doctor, as you waste your time drawing and painting."

That day, I felt very discouraged, because there were only three months left for our major exam. I was very sensitive to others' opinions and assessments of me because I valued others' opinions of me more than my own opinion. I went home feeling rejected.

My dad saw me and he was very in tune with our moods, so he asked me: "Sobia, are you okay?" I told him, "Papa, I feel like I will not be able to fulfill your expectations and I will not score well in my exams." I explained what Mrs. K said, and I never forgot what he said that day. "Sobia, you are the most brilliant girl I have ever seen. She can only see the tip of the iceberg. You and only you know about your true potential. Please don't let her faulty perception of you discourage you. Remember in this world, you set your own appraisal."

Those words stuck in my mind. You set your own appraisal. That means all what the world gives back to you is a reflection of your own self-esteem. My dad then went to our library, took out a very tiny book and handed it to me. The book was called Psycho-Cybernetics, written by a plastic surgeon Maxwell Maltz, which describes the self-image and how to use visualization to change your self-image.

Since I am a right brain dominant person and I used to daydream a lot, practicing these visualizations was a piece of cake for me. In fact, I enjoyed the visualization techniques so much that I practiced them almost an hour a day. I visualized myself doing great in all my subjects, including math. I redefined my self-image. I visualized my name on the honor board of my school where each year the name of the student who stood first in the whole school is written. These visualizations and positive frame of mind gave me the energy to study day and night.

These visualizations and positive frame of mind gave me the energy to study day and night. As part of my visualizations, I created a vision board, which I divided into three sections. In the middle section, I created a painting of myself holding an award stating "Sobia Yaqub, 1st position, Azam Garrison School." On one side of the board, I created an hourly timetable for the next 3 months, outlining the steps to achieving my goal. On the final section, I wrote a poem. Each section contributed to my larger goal of achieving a place on that honor board.

"Yes, I am a loving and creative soul,
I am an artist who is driven by my passion.
And by the Grace of God, I will become a doctor by profession.
And with my knowledge I will help people,
as elevating others is my obsession."
– Dr. Sobia Yaqub

I wanted to prove to my math teacher that she was wrong in her perception of me and at the same time I wanted to make my parents proud of me.

"The best revenge is massive success."
– Frank Sinatra

Finally, I took my exams. The results came in and I stood first in the whole school, among about 150 girls in the 10th grade. My name and picture were published in the newspaper. I got into the best college in Pakistan, Kinnard college, and then went to the medical school I dreamt of. It was the same medical school my sisters graduated from. I became a firm believer in the power of visualization. I met Mrs. K in the school in the principal's office, where she told me, "Sobia, we are proud of you."

It all happened because I didn't believe in her limited perception of me. I believed in my own vision and my God-given abilities. I valued my own assessment of myself more than how she assessed me.

Do you find yourself bound by cultural expectations? Have you allowed those expectations to impact how you perceive yourself? Cultural expectations have a way of hemming us in, giving us a reason to judge ourselves harshly, often without real cause. When you explore your passions and find the things that bring you joy, that might not meet the expectations of your culture or society as a whole.

Per Dr. Wayne Dyer, the people who get the most approval from the world are the people who need others' approval the least. It is very important to understand the concept. A person with good self-esteem does not need approval from other people, as his own approval is enough for him. It is similar to a person who leaves home after having a heavy breakfast. He isn't looking for restaurants to go eat at because he is already full.

Let's look at how you describe yourself to others. What qualities do you think of first? Are they negative ones, or do you focus on your positive attributes first? It can be easy to slip into a negative state of mind, focusing on the things you need to improve or the areas in which you feel you fall short.

Self-esteem, in simple terms, is basically about how you see yourself, what you expect from yourself that dictates how you carry yourself in this world, and ultimately has indirect control on how others treat you and how you take advantage of your circumstances, rather than allowing circumstances and people to take advantage of you.

I got married, and soon after, I landed in New York in January 2001. My husband and I lived in Manhattan. I came across many individuals who would tell me that they couldn't understand my foreign accent. Had I not believed in myself and carried a healthy self-esteem, I would never have been chosen as a physician coach by my organization. Part of my position included coaching other physicians in different primary care settings.

Can you believe it? I have been coaching the physicians who were born and raised in the United States, helping them to learn how to communicate with the American patients on a one-to-one level. On top of that, I was getting paid for my coaching services. I had to use my visualization practices to overcome many hurdles in my life, but I have also enjoyed many opportunities as a result.

When I was recognized as the "The Women of the Year 2017," I took my parents with me to the pride of performance award ceremony in Anaheim, California. They were called on stage as well. When we came down after receiving the award, my mom said, "Sobia , I am proud of you. You pursued your passions along with your career, and today you were recognized for helping others with your God-gifted passions."

I believe all of us have a calling and a purpose hidden deep inside, and only we can discover what our calling is. I auction my art work and all the profits go to my nonprofit charitable organization. It gives me fulfillment. We need to find ways to fulfill our souls.

I am not advocating for you to have an inflated sense of yourself, to the point that you can't see areas where you need to improve or want to better yourself. Instead, I want you to avoid the other extreme, where you are so hard on yourself that it is mentally and emotionally damaging. When you reach that point, you can't help yourself or others. You end up shortchanging the world because deny your gifts, talents, and abilities, and you don't allow your unique contribution to be felt.

Think of all the ways that you talk to yourself on a daily basis; the mental dialogue that you have and the points you choose to focus on. When you are presented with negative situations or less than ideal circumstances, do you see them as an opportunity for growth or do you see them as another reason to be down on yourself? Focusing on how you are not meeting specific expectations can be a key to bringing yourself down and creating an internal dialogue that damages you.

When you get into a negative loop, you are devaluing yourself. You are choosing to define yourself as damaged goods of little value. Others may see your value and be frustrated at why you don't see it as well. They are not privy to all the thoughts in your head, the ones that focus on all the ways you don't measure up. It can be hard to find your value with that type of dialogue on constant repeat.

Still, I want you to start the process of changing that inner dialogue by focusing on replacing one negative thought with a positive one. For instance, if you are focusing on some aspects of your appearance that you don't like and wish you could improve, then find one part of your physical appearance that you are proud of and focus on that. Internally, you need to remind yourself about those unique aspects of yourself that are your contributions to the world. Be thankful for them.

Be mindful of how you talk to yourself about who you are. Negative thinking can become so pervasive that you don't even realize that you are doing it. Instead, that negative internal dialogue becomes a record that is stuck in one groove, never moving forward. Being mindful means consciously taking the time to examine what you are telling yourself, and making changes based on those assessments.

Time and again, you will find that when you consciously focus on that internal dialogue, you can start to pick up on those negative trains of thought that are limiting you and causing damage to how you view yourself.

I will be talking about being mindful throughout these pages, because I want you to recognize that too many things you tell yourself are there because you created an unconscious habit. You will have to be mindfully aware, in order to change that habit and create a new one to take its place. Your mindset needs to shift from the negative to the positive, and that starts by recognizing your value and then focusing on how your value is a gift to the world.

CHANGING THE DIALOGUE MEANS CHANGING YOUR MINDSET

I find that the first thing I have to recognize is that I do have value. Not just as a spouse, daughter, and mother, but as an individual. The world is richer because I am alive in it, and the world is richer because of you as well. Each of us has value, and brings a special talent, a unique gift with us as our contribution to making the world a better place.

When you talk to yourself, focus on what you can offer to others, not what you can't. Focusing on the negative without a clear plan to address it is a sure way to bring down your sense of self and create a mindset of complaining, negativity, and hopelessness.

Part of what can help you to change that mindset is to make a conscious effort each day to focus on a positive aspect of your life, and who you are as an individual. The reason that this is so critical is that every day you are being bombarded with the negative. It is on the news, on television, and on the radio. Social media is full of information that focuses on how you don't measure up.

When you make a conscious effort to focus on a positive in your life, you are shifting the internal dialogue away from the negative. Start with a mantra on a daily basis. It could be a mantra of something that you are thankful for. Every day you need to think of something different. Don't just start the day by saying you are thankful for the same thing over and over. Then it becomes something you do by rote and it does not carry the same value over time.

Instead, choose to be mindful about the things that you appreciate in your life. It could be a gift of patience, or the ability to help others through food, music, or a listening ear. You might be thankful for the ability to work and provide for yourself and your family. No matter what you choose to be thankful for, be in the moment and give meaningful thanks for that gift, ability, or circumstance.

Even if you are going through a difficult period in your life, find a reason to be thankful. When you are grieving the loss of a loved one, it can be hard to find that reason to be thankful. But it is there in the memories you have.

You clearly are thankful for the moments that you can look back on, that can make you smile.

My point is not that you will not have painful circumstances in your life, but that you need to look beyond the moment to find the reason for thankfulness, or to find how you can benefit from those circumstances.

I know that during my immigration to the U.S., I had to find reasons for joy and thankfulness, even as my world was shifting. The culture was different, how individuals viewed the world was different, and I had to adapt. I had to recognize that my gift was empathy and the ability to see a person, not just as a body to be healed, but as a person who needed my knowledge and skill to mend their mind, body, and spirit. It gave me a unique perspective, one that others valued, and resulted in my assignment to train other doctors on how to deal with patients.

As a doctor, I have to think of the whole person, not just one part or another. When you are talking about your own value, you need to see all of your value, not just one or two things. It is not about focusing on a few nuggets but seeing all the amazing facets of who you are.

I believe that it is critical to have empathy for others, recognizing that they may be dealing with the difficult parts of their own journey. At the same time, however, you need to have empathy for yourself. You might be willing to give someone else a pass because they are grieving a loss, but you don't do the same for yourself. If you get nothing else from this chapter, I want you to hear this: Be kind to yourself!

Part of improving your self-image involves not only focusing on areas of your life where you can be grateful but concentrating on the positive aspects of your life. There are going to be things that you wish you could change or that you want to be different, but the reality is that you do not need to dwell on them to the point that they bring you down to a level of seeing yourself as less than.

START WITH VISUALIZATION

You can start to improve your self-image by using a tool known as visualization. It is important to realize that your mind has powerful abilities to create and shift your reality. When you make a conscious effort to visualize a different path for yourself, and you do so on a daily basis, you will start to see circumstances shift in your daily life.

Let's think about this in terms of cars. If you are interested in purchasing a new car, you might do research on a specific model or various bells and whistles. Then you might begin to notice those types of cars are everywhere. Did that car really become more popular, or are you more aware of it now because you are interested in purchasing one?

The point here is that what you dwell on mentally becomes part of your reality. If you want to change how you view yourself, then you need to dwell on the positive aspects of your personality, on your goals, and on what you offer to others. As you make a conscious effort to visualize these things, then you will find it easier to acknowledge them in your reality.

The benefits of visualization are vast. Visualization can help you to accelerate your goals and dreams, simply because it gives you a means to be hyper-focused, and confident in your ability to achieve your goals. Using visualization, you can stimulate your creative side, allowing yourself to come up with creative methods to achieve your goals. Too often, individuals find themselves stuck, because they have a goal but no clear way to achieve it.

Creative thinking takes you out of the box, but also gives you the means to come up with ideas or methods that might not have occurred to you before.

Part of visualization involves reprogramming your brain, helping you to recognize resources that can assist you. Like the car, once you are focused on something, your subconscious will draw your attention to resources that you might not have noticed before. I find that it is easier to find what you need when you are focused on it and your brain is giving it top priority. Visualization is a way for you to put order to your brain's input, helping your conscious and subconscious mind to recognize the priorities and then bring them to your attention.

At this point, any discussion of visualization would be meaningless if I did not discuss the law of attraction. Simply put, the law of attraction is one of the most powerful laws in the universe. You attract into your life what you focus on. Whatever you give your time, energy, and attention to will then be attracted into your life. If you are positive and focused on things that give you joy and excitement, you will draw more of those things into your life.

The same is true of negative energy. When you send it out, you are going to receive it back. Now let's apply this to your self-image. If you are focused on the negative aspects of your self-image, you will see more of them. You are attracting that negativity. However, if you decide to focus on the positive aspects of your self-image, you will draw more of those positives into your life.

According to Jack Canfield, "The Law of Attraction allows for infinite possibilities, infinite abundance, and infinite joy. It knows no order of difficulty, and it can change your life in every way."

When you choose to think differently about situations, when you choose what to focus on, and when you choose to respond differently, you will draw different experiences and responses in return. You have the ability to choose your future, to participate in creating the life you want. It all starts by visualizing it, and training your brain to work in harmony with those visualizations.

Notice that the point is to ask for and focus on what you want, not what you don't want. Shifting your focus through visualization is key to having the impact you want through the Law of Attraction.

Finally, visualization is going to help you get excited about achieving your goals and objectives. You are motivating yourself to achieve your dreams and to build the life that you want, one that gives you purpose and allows you to leave a legacy for others.

Here are a few visualization techniques that you can put into practice in your life. Once you start making a habit of them, you will be able to benefit more fully from the effects.

• Start by making it a daily practice. Those who attain the most with visualization start by taking a few minutes each day to rehearse what they want to accomplish. Doing so daily keeps it fresh in your mind and creates that hyper-focus you need to achieve it.

• Give it detail. Part of the effectiveness of visualization is that you are creating a detailed image that your brain can focus on making your reality. To make it more real, you need to focus on sharpening every aspect of your goal. Imagine your clothing, your facial expressions, the colors, sounds, and even how things might feel. Include your own feelings, to give the visualization real depth.

• Put yourself into that moment and infuse it throughout your body. Give yourself complete power to touch, smell, taste, see, and hear. The more real it is in your visualization, the more your brain will want to make it your reality.

Throughout these points, I was essentially teaching you about the power of creation that you have. In fact, we all have this ability, but so few of us take the time to use it effectively. Negative self-image can play a big part in why individuals are not using their powers of creation effectively. Instead, they focus on what is not going right and as a result, they draw more of the same into their lives.

Let's shift this discussion to your self-image. Are you always focusing on what you do wrong, on the ways that you "fail" at what you try to do? I am not talking about healthy self-analysis, where you look at your actions with an eye on continuous improvement. I am talking about beating yourself up for how you reacted, how you behaved, or how you didn't achieve as much as you had hoped. When you focus strictly on the negative, you are going to find yourself making more mistakes and drawing more of that negativity into your life.

Have you ever had a really bad day? We all have. As the day goes along, the more you focus on what has already gone wrong, the more that seems to go wrong. It becomes a vicious cycle, one that can be hard to break. However, with a conscious effort, you can break that cycle. Now think of your life in the large sense. You have the capability to break the cycle of negativity in your life and create something different.

To make your visualization even more powerful, use pictures of yourself accomplishing your goal. Doing so can help you give that detail to your visualizations that can help you to truly see it. No matter what goal you have in your life, be it financial, career, recreation, or experiences you want to have, visualization can be critical to successfully bringing it to fruition.

To support your visualizations, it is important to use affirmations. They are helpful in reinforcement, because they evoke not only the picture of what you want, but also the experience of already having what you want. When you repeat an affirmation several times a day, it strengthens your motivation and programs your subconscious to do whatever it takes to make that goal or objective a reality.

As you can see, using visualizations and affirmations enable you to change your beliefs, assumptions, and opinions. Harness your brain to create the results you want, and harness your ability into a purposeful direction.

Make sure that your visualizations and affirmations are part of your daily routine. It is best to do them mornings and evenings. However, you don't want to spend the whole day thinking only of your goals, because then you won't be able to enjoy the moment. You may find that you are more willing to take chances and seize opportunities when you have a regular routine of visualization and affirmations. Daily routines can help you to stay balanced and allow you to appreciate the life that you have right now, as well as work towards the one you want to have in the future.

Your mental focus will shift to what you want to achieve, and you will have less time to focus on any negativity that may filter into your life from time to time by circumstances out of your control.

ACT WITH YOUR CIRCUMSTANCES

Throughout your life, you are going to be presented with circumstances that are beyond your control. The loss of a loved one, unexpected natural disasters, or even a sudden illness can all negatively impact your life. However, you can choose your reaction, and how those circumstances impact you.

100

Our self-esteem is conveyed consciously, and largely unconsciously, through subliminal stimuli. Based on studies, 95% of our brain activity is beyond our awareness, and that is where our self-esteem lies. Only 5% of our brain activity is conscious. The way we stand, the way we sit, the way we talk, the way we breathe, the tone of voice and the words we choose, the way we make eye contact, and the way we shake hands are all dictated by our self-esteem, and all of them teach people how to treat us. Our conscious and unconscious thoughts are in constant communication with the universe.

Not that you won't have an emotional response, but you can choose to take that emotional response and channel it towards your benefit. I find that every difficult circumstance presents me with an opportunity to bring my best self to the table. I can take it and use it as a learning opportunity, instead of a reason to stop trying to achieve in my life or move forward.

Your thoughts trigger emotions, and your emotions are often the trigger for your actions. When you take a moment to consciously control your thoughts about a situation or circumstance, you are taking control of your emotions and, thereby, your actions. Remember too, that when you choose your reaction, you are choosing what you want to focus on and are giving the Law of Attraction the information that it needs to bring things into your life.

Most of this will start with shifting your vibrations. What do I mean by this? It means that you need to focus on creating positive emotions in the world, including joy, love, peace, and appreciation. When you practice feeling these emotions, and creating these emotions with your thoughts, you are going to change your vibration.

Once you do that, you will start to notice that your reality begins to match that positive vibration. You will draw to yourself more of what you are putting out in terms of positive energy. Granted, you might not feel joy every day.

However, it is important to stop negative emotions in their tracks. If you aren't feeling joyful, then visualize circumstances where you did feel joyful and bring that feeling into the moment.

Many individuals focus on what they don't want, and then wonder why they are not achieving everything that they imagine is possible for their lives. The reason is that the Law of Attraction is going to bring what you focus on, either positive or negative. Therefore, it is key to focus on what you want to achieve and then act to back it up. When you do so, you allow your unique contribution to benefit yourself and others.

At this moment, I want to shift the discussion away from how you benefit from the Law of Attraction and instead focus on how you can use it to help others.

I have spent a lot of time talking about the importance of positive thinking, bringing positive energy into your life by choosing what to focus on, and I have given you some techniques to help you bring your thoughts and actions in line with what you want to achieve. Now I want to talk about how you can use that to help others.

Remember, you can't choose your circumstances, but you can choose how to react to them. Your example can be an inspiration to others who are looking for a way to deal with their own challenging circumstances. When they see how you handle your challenges, they are likely to want to gain a deeper understanding of what you are doing to achieve your results.

The treatment of low or faulty self-esteem incorporates a wide variety of methods and techniques, including visualization, neuro-linguistic programming (NLP), hypnosis, and psychology, and the treatment varies based on each individual. Some individuals may even need pharmaceutical intervention to temporarily address symptoms of anxiety that may arise as my patients embark on a new journey of behaving in a certain way.

THE BENEFITS OF MENTORING

Serving as a mentor for someone can help them to gain knowledge and experiences that they might otherwise have missed. Your legacy can often be wrapped up in what you do for others, how you help them to achieve their own goals, how you inspire them to think creatively about their situation, and how you give them something to reach for in their lives.

Success tends to breed a better sense of self-image, because positive experiences feed positive thinking, which draws more positive experiences your way. That positive self-image is reflected in how you treat others and will impact how they react to you. What you put out into the universe comes back to you.

All of us have a purpose, one that allows us to have a positive impact on others. Your self-image is going to impact how much you are able to assist others, inspire them, or provide mentorship. You have the capability to build more than you have ever imagined possible, and it starts by focusing on what you want to build and then acting in accordance with your vision.

What gets you excited to get up in the morning? Think of all the different activities or events that bring you joy as you participate in them. Are there ways that you are able to dignify others by your actions? I often think of the proverb, "There is more happiness in giving than in receiving." The reason I want to bring this up is because when you help others, it positively impacts your own self-image.

When you feel your self-image improving, it motivates you to step outside of your comfort zone. Perhaps you have an idea for a business that will solve a problem in your community, while providing sustainable jobs for individuals looking for work. When you are in a negative vein of thinking, your actions reflect that negativity, and you will talk yourself out of pursuing that idea.

Yet, when you shift your internal dialogue, suddenly, you are able to see how your idea could work and you see any obstacles as challenges instead of roadblocks. My point is that your self-image can either block you from moving forward, or it can be the catalyst that starts you on a path to achieving your purpose and impacting others.

At this point, I want to focus on a simple principle that is critical to your success. Whatever you think about, whatever you make your focus, is what you will bring into your life. Acknowledging this fact can help you to recognize your own power to create and help you to work in harmony with that power to achieve your life purpose.

As part of that effort, I want you to look for a mentor, one who can help you to think outside the box and hold you accountable when you are allowing negative thinking to dominate. When I work with individuals, I help them to see how critical their own internal dialogue is to their success. When I speak to myself with an empathic voice, truly recognize my legitimate concerns, and then work to address them, I see myself reaching the goals and dreams that I set for myself.

I want to help you to achieve that as well. Your vision is unique to you, and the world needs that unique vision. We can all sit down and create a laundry list of items that need to be fixed or changed in the world. Complaining about it rarely results in true change, but just leads to more negative energy. I want to spark a change in you, one that can help us all to shift the energy from negative to positive.

As part of your visualization and affirmations, it is important to recognize that what you are creating in your own reality has ripple effects across a much larger pond. Circling back to how your actions can impact others, you need to recognize that the energy you use to create your reality will help you to inspire or bring down others. The choice is truly up to you.

Everything that you do when it comes to creating positive energy in your life is going to take practice. You aren't going to wake up one day with a brand-new self-image and a completely different way of talking to yourself. Instead, you are going to have to make a conscious decision and then keep practicing on a daily basis.

I am a firm believer that you get what you expect out of life, with the help of God. This is my passion, to help you live your life at your peak potential. This can only happen if you redefine your self-esteem and let go of the wrong labels that were put on you by ignorant people. Don't let anyone else design your life. Only you have the right to estimate your worth. The only way to get to where you want to go is to have the insight of where you are, and to redefine your self-image and change your internal representation. Otherwise, it is like navigating the world with the wrong map in your hands.

As you practice, you are creating new patterns of thinking, and new habits. Your brain will learn and, eventually, a positive frame of mind and self-image will become the norm. It will be your default position. I look forward to helping you achieve the self-image that allows you to benefit others with your unique contribution, while allowing you to achieve your life's purpose!

For more information about Dr. Sobia Yaqub, please go to www.Doctoryslifecoaching.com or you can call Dr. Sobia directly at 972-325-8205.

What Does Change Mean to You?

Fundamental Elements for a Vibrant, Fulfilling Life

TONY DEBOGORSKI

How do you view change? For many individuals, change has become something to fear. It invokes feelings of anxiety and potential loss. There is often little focus on what we can gain from change. Instead, the negative feelings and thought patterns overwhelm us, which can make change more difficult to accept and benefit from.

Think of the flight or fight response. Change, if we don't manage it effectively, can trigger that response. It can make us respond as if our lives are being threatened, when it's more likely that we are simply being affected by changing circumstances. Some of these circumstances are in our control and others are out of our control. However, if we can alter our reaction to change, then we can reap some amazing benefits.

Yes, you can benefit from change. However, in order to do so you need to be willing to create a new mindset in regards to how you view change and how you choose to act. Without the right mindset, you might be missing out on a change that could give depth to your life and the lives of those around you.

Changes, both those that happen to us and the ones that we create ourselves, have the potential to create new opportunities and experiences we might otherwise miss. These can give us another perspective and enrich our lives. Change did just that for me as a young man.

I grew up in rural Canada, where hard work and sweat were the building blocks of your success. I learned to be a jack of all trades, because that was the way you got things done around a farm. When I left to attend university, the idea was that I would end up coming home, marrying my high school girlfriend, and raising my family in the farming community where I was raised.

This step towards a university education was already a big change, since only a few of my family members actually went on to get a university education. Working hard was our way of life, and it was hard physical work. I couldn't imagine any other way, but university gave me a new way to live and introduced me to the idea of working smarter, not harder.

My life was enriched by not only the classes I attended, but the people I met. I was exposed to those who hadn't lived their entire life on a farm.

I was exposed to different perspectives on how to tackle a variety of challenges. It altered my perception of the world, giving me a broader viewpoint. At the same time, I also deepened my appreciation of the values my parents instilled in me.

It was my first experience with change, but definitely not my last. I took the step to open my mind to change, which allowed me to get comfortable with the idea. During this time, I learned that it was okay to find assistance in accepting a change and acting on it without fear. The life I live today is defined by change. Now, instead of fear and anxiety, I welcome change for the blessings it may bring. How did I get to this point? It started with my willingness to learn and grew from there.

There is a process to change, but if we are not careful, we can actually prolong the process and make it more difficult. Let's walk through the reality of change. First, you have the old status quo. This is the reality of how things are right now. It could be a fairly peaceful way of life or you could find it difficult, but it is what you know.

Now a foreign element is introduced. It could be a new job or a move, for example. Most of the time, our first reaction is to resist, fearing the chaos that we are sure is to follow. After a point, we see the transforming idea of change and begin to integrate it into our lives. As time goes on, we then integrate the change into our lives and thus create a new status quo. Still, the impact of many aspects of this process can be lessened if we take a different point of view toward change.

Through mentors and my own experiences, I learned the key elements that can impact your ability to not only weather change, but thrive in the process. These five key elements are necessary to create the right mindset, one that embraces change, instead of being governed by a fear of change.

KEY #1. SELF-BELIEF

The first key is your belief in yourself. This is the foundation of a vibrant and fulfilling life. Without confidence in your own ability to handle challenges, you will see change as a crisis, instead of a benefit or an opportunity to grow as an individual.

Throughout our lives, we are told how to act, dress, and even think. Our belief systems are influenced by this training. In addition, as we grow older and other influences come into play from the world around us. Just take a moment and think about all the people and ideas you encounter on a daily basis. These could be teachers, family members, workmates, television, the internet, etc. The list goes on and on.

All of these influences are not focused on teaching us to think for ourselves, but instead are focused on developing our thinking to fall in line with who they believe we should be. Call it the social conditioning of our world. There often isn't time to learn who we are, to spend time with ourselves, to think, imagine, and explore the world. Instead, if we don't buy out the time, we can find that we are dissatisfied with our lives and unable to determine why.

We often have our purpose in life defined for us by others. This can lead to a lack of fulfillment in our lives, especially if what we are supposed to be doesn't fit our true vision of who we are.

The key is to stop and examine your belief system. Focus on your values.

How many of them would you say you genuinely believe and how many have you taken on because of someone else in your life? It is amazing how many of our beliefs may no longer be serving us, but we are still using them to define ourselves and the world around us. Like the traditional fall and spring cleaning of our homes, we need to constantly be willing to clean the beliefs that no longer serve us or contribute to the growth and happiness of our lives from our consciousness.

Do you wake up in the morning satisfied with where you are in life? Can you look in the mirror and see a face excited to meet the day? Do you feel accountable for your life or does it feel as if your life is happening to you? How you see the world is based on your self-belief. What crafts your self-belief?

It hinges on your ability to see yourself master a skill and then be able to do it again and again successfully. Positive experiences help us grow our confidence in ourselves and define who we are. These moments often start in our early childhood, setting up a pattern throughout our lives.

My first memory of confidence building occurred when I was 11 years old. The regional elementary track and field meet was coming up. I wanted to win the top male athlete award. Although I had participated in the meet in the past, I hadn't won before. This time, I decided to do things differently. In preparation for the meet, I spent extra time training, including running after school. I was determined and my goal dominated my thoughts. It was a type of visualization, one that helped build my confidence going into the meet.

I had entered into five events and there were points for coming into first, second, and third place. On the day of the meet, it was sunny, the field and track were dry. Conditions were perfect for this outdoor event. My focus was on doing my best to earn the most points possible. At the end of the event, I had four first place ribbons and one for second place. I was presented with the trophy for top male athlete. That feeling of accomplishment boosted my sense of what I could do and built my self-belief.

What goals have you set that you were able to accomplish on your own? How did you feel after you achieved your goal? Setting and accomplishing goals is a great way to feel better about yourself. How does this translate into having a different mindset about change? When you feel confidence in your abilities, you will not find yourself fearing change and the challenges it can present.

However, in the midst of a major change, you might find yourself neglecting your needs. How often do we put ourselves last when others around us are in need of our time and attention? While we might think that it will last for only a short period of time, putting ourselves on the back burner can become a routine, one that has a negative impact on our lives.

This can leave you worn out mentally and put you into a negative frame of mind. I can point to research and personal experiences to give you examples of why a negative mindset can be the anti-change and can encourage you to avoid thinking about the potential benefits of change. Once you focus on caring for your needs, you are in a better position to weather change and give assistance to others. Once you find confidence and strength in yourself and your abilities, you will be able to master whatever change and challenges come your way.

One important point is that you might still be afraid, but don't let it paralyze you into not acting at all. Remember those moments of success and allow them to motivate you to keep going. The keys to being self-reliant are perseverance, dedication, and integrity. When you have them, you will be able to conquer just about anything.

KEY #2. PURPOSE

Your life is a journey and you are the navigator. Some individuals choose to navigate based on their surroundings, essentially letting the waves aimlessly lead them along. In the end, that kind of life rarely leads to happiness with change or with yourself. You become a product of your circumstances, instead of defining yourself on your own terms.

What is purpose? According to the American Heritage Dictionary, it is "The object toward which one strives or for which something exists, an aim or a goal. The reason for which anything is done, created or exists, an aim or a goal."

When you examine your own life, are you excited about what you do? Could you define the purpose of your life? For some, their purpose becomes apparent when they are young. They find the passion that defines their lives and shapes their careers. Others never find that purpose, leaving them to struggle to find satisfaction with their lives.

If you haven't defined the purpose of your life, then it is time to think about what you enjoy. What sparks your passion? What gets you excited to get out of bed in the morning? Once you start to define your purpose, set your goals around what you enjoy. This can help you gain perspective on your purpose.

However, keep in mind that your purpose is not set in stone. It can change over time as you gain life experience and a better understanding of yourself. Taking action will help you be drawn to what you like. Try new things. Consider the spiritual influences in your life. To postulate is the act of creation. It can happen when you think, write, or speak something into being. Focus, because if you think it, then you can do it.

Change can be initiated by you. It doesn't have to be dominated by circumstances outside of your control. You can start by taking one action that will move you closer to a specific goal. That goal could be to simply change your way of thinking or to release a belief that is no longer serving you, but could be limiting you instead.

With your purpose defined, you could move forward to produce the life you want and mindset for change, which starts with how you take care of yourself.

KEY #3. HEALTH

Fear and anxiety can have physical repercussions. They impact how our bodies feel, as well as our ability to fight off illnesses and deal with chronic conditions. Research has proven time and again that our minds can influence our physical well-being.

Are you poisoning your body through the negative thoughts you are dwelling on? To create the energy necessary for a vibrant fulfilling life you need to maximize your mental state, maintain your physical body, and nourish yourself properly. Keep your mind focused on what is possible, instead of focusing on what can't be done or any potentially negative consequences.

The combination of your mind and body is a synergistic relationship. It means you need to take care of both to achieve overall well-being. To start, let's focus on your physical body. Are you getting out on a regular basis to exercise and stretch your muscles? Do you raise your heart rate? One of the interesting side effects of physical activity is how it can impact our mood. When we are uplifted in mood, it translates into our thought processes. Regular physical exercise can contribute to greater overall positivity in our lives.

If you find it hard to get out on your own and get physically active, then consider finding a support group, a partner, or even a gym where you can be held accountable for showing up and putting in the effort. You will appreciate the results in terms of your health, making it worth the effort. Additionally, the physical benefits will allow you to grow in other areas of your life, thus making change more welcome, especially as your body grows stronger.

When it comes to your physical well-being, the reality is that you are what you put into your body. If you don't fuel your body for optimal performance, then it can't give you the very best physically. That can have a domino effect on how you operate mentally. When you are tired and not feeling your best, can you honestly say that you have made your best decisions? Or do you find yourself rethinking those choices at a later date?

There are five products, which I refer to as the five white poisons, that you need to be aware of. They can be found in a variety of foods throughout your local grocery store. So much of what we eat today has been processed extensively, removing the natural nutrients and fiber-rich parts. As a result, we are exposed to more of these five products than ever before. What are these five white poisons? Sugar, starch, flour, salt, and milk.

All of these are foods that need to be consumed in moderation. Recognize that they are often hidden ingredients within other foods. Therefore, it is wise to limit your intake wherever possible to make sure you aren't putting too much of these items into your body.

Part of your physical health is also caring for your brain. Think of it as a muscle. Like every muscle in your body, it is important to allow it to relax and get the necessary rest. This can be done through meditation or even finding some quiet time away from your family and friends to relax and think quietly without distraction. Doing so also allows you to reduce your stress level. Making sure your stress level comes down will positively impact your mental health as well.

Do you have a place that brings you peace? Having this place allows you to mentally unwind and just let go of your stress, even if it is just temporarily. Meditation is a method that you can use, even if all you can do is go to a quiet place in your home or office. There are a variety of meditation techniques available. Some individuals prefer a calming form of music to accompany their meditation, while others prefer to just enjoy the silence. Whatever you prefer, the point is to make your mental health a priority. If you do, it will be much easier to handle change and thrive.

Change can bring benefits and give us opportunities we might not otherwise have considered without the upheaval in our lives. But in order to benefit from change, we need to maintain our positivity, both physically and mentally. This can be hard to do when a change has a particularly emotional impact. Relying on family and friends for support is key to dealing with the more emotional aspects of any change in your life.

Throughout this discussion of your health, I haven't really touched on one area that impacts our well-being. That is our relationships. But how do they impact our lives and what do we need to remember about these relationships when it comes to change?

KEY #4. RELATIONSHIPS

Did you know that you are shaped by the people you spend the most time with? Those individuals will influence your ideas, beliefs, and actions. This also extends to your attitude. If you are surrounded by positive thinkers, it is much easier to maintain a positive attitude. Think about the last time you were surrounded by negative individuals. After a while, did it seem as if that negative and critical spirit rubbed off on you?

Here are some questions to ask yourself about the people you spend time with. Are they primarily positive or negative? Do you find yourself having spirited conversations with plenty of give and take, or do you find that you are just a dumping ground for all their complaints about life?

If you want to create change in your life or be more accepting of the changes in your life, then you may need to assess who you spend most of your time with. Creating a new attitude or shifting your thought process means assessing who is influencing them both and whether that influence is helping or hurting.

When I was finishing my university education, I was associating with a group of friends who were eager to join the corporate world. I had worked in the corporate world during my summer breaks, but I had also started a business installing sprinkler systems in areas where there was new home construction. I did this after hours and on weekends. Although I was working a lot, I was also figuring out that I didn't have to go the corporate route to be successful. My small part-time business had made me more money than my daily corporate job.

Our final year of school came and, of course, my friends and I discussed what our next steps were as we started life after university. Some had mixed feelings about what direction to take after graduating. The options included attempting to open a business in the role of entrepreneur or applying to one of the many companies out there for a traditional corporate role.

Since most of my friends decided to go the corporate route, I did too, even though my experience indicated that I could be equally, if not more, successful in the role of entrepreneur. The individuals I associated with provided acknowledgement and support during that decision-making period of my life.

Are there some decisions where you can see the influence of your associates? Can you look back now and see that perhaps a different decision would have been more appropriate for the path you ultimately wanted to pursue?

While we all want to think that we are independent thinkers, sudden influences from our associates can impact what we choose to do and how we think and act. Yet, with a greater understanding of who you are as a person (your goals and your passions), you will find that you can truly be an independent thinker and identify the effect of those influences around you.

Self-knowledge takes time, but the reward is a better way to embrace life and the change around us, both personally and professionally. If you want to move down a specific path toward your goal, you need to make sure to associate with like-minded individuals. They can encourage and support you as you work to achieve those specific milestones.

As you discover what you are passionate about, you will be able to find like-minded friends and associates who are focused on that particular activity or pursuit. For instance, you may be passionate about helping young people. There may be local groups geared toward providing activities and mentorship to teenagers within your community. Getting involved in those groups will put you around others who share your passion, which can help motivate you even further.

Take the time to examine your beliefs and determine if the friends you are associating with are the right people to support you in the next stage or season of your life. Not everyone you spend time with will be an active part of helping you achieve your goals. However, they can be the individuals who make you laugh, as well as help you see the positive when situations or circumstances seem overwhelming.

The point is to be around people who embrace change and can help you to do the same. When it comes to your mindset, negative association will eventually bring even the most positive mindset down. Have you ever tried to accomplish something that you had already decided was impossible? It becomes an uphill battle, and you likely didn't succeed.

A positive attitude, on the other hand, makes it possible for you to achieve even more than you thought was possible. In addition, your positive mindset could have an influence on those around you. Imagine being a positive influence to those who are important to you. The best relationships are the ones where you both are actively working to support and encourage each other in pursuit of your passions, while being there for each other during times of major change or upheaval that life seems to throw at us all.

If you are looking to make adjustments to your circle of friends and associates, consider looking into your community for opportunities to meet new people. Some ideas include joining a club or charity organization. If there is an activity that you have been interested in trying, why not sign up for lessons? What things have you been afraid to try for one reason or another? Why not give one of those things a try? If your fear is that you won't do well, make peace with that and do it anyway. You might find that as you conquer your fear, you make new friends that will enrich your life.

I want to point out here that the idea is to make you better able to adapt to change and train yourself to see the benefit of change versus focusing on the fear and anxiety. Each of these new experiences is putting you in charge of creating change in your life on a smaller scale, which will make it easier for you to handle change on a larger scale.

The most rewarding sport even for me was signing up and participating in triathlons. I was a prairie boy who didn't grow up around water. Signing up for a triathlon forced me to learn how to swim. I could have let fear of the unknown stop me, but instead I broadened my horizons.

Additionally, I signed up with a friend. We challenged each other and held each other accountable for attaining our goals. It was not an easy journey, but I found new strength as I pushed myself and supported my friend.

The 10-month journey before my first triathlon was grueling at times. It included swim lessons, getting the proper equipment, the proper bike, the right shoes, and more. After those 10 months of training, lessons, and standing up to my own fears, the day of the race finally came.

The first leg of the triathlon was swimming, which I can definitely say was not my strength. In fact, when I ran into the water, I was with a pack of men, but after a few minutes of kicking and banging around, I was alone and about ready to give up. Instead of doing that, I pulled back for a moment, composed myself, and then started to swim, concentrating on one stroke at a time.

I finished dead last in the swim, but at least I finished. I continued with ease to do the bike and run, completing those two legs in top times. I was dead last overall, because of my slow swim, but I still felt a great sense of accomplishment because I had completed my goal. In the process, I had met many new people who shared an interest in triathlons. I also got closer to my friend Nick, who trained with me and completed the same triathlon.

It was a rewarding event for me, not only because I actually finished what I set out to do, but because when I went out to celebrate that night, I met my future wife. Our relationship has been full of change and challenges, but none of the joys would have been possible if I hadn't stepped outside of my comfort zone to try something new and conquered a fear at the same time.

Think about the various relationships in your life. Could there be someone who is already in your life who would be supportive as you step outside your comfort zone? Those individuals are the ones who will support you through change. They are key relationships to nurture. Still, those relationships will not be able to support you if you are not able to communicate your needs to those critical people in your life. As a result, my fifth key is also the most critical: communication.

KEY #5. COMMUNICATION

No matter who we are and what we do throughout the day, we are constantly communicating. We use our faces, our hands, and, of course, our speech to communicate what we are thinking and feeling on a daily basis.

Yet within the realm of communication, the opportunities for misunderstandings abound. There are literally hundreds of thousands of examples throughout history demonstrating how misunderstandings can grow into much larger breakdowns of relationships between individuals, groups, and even countries.

Communication is truly an incredible concept. Great communicators can wow us and bring difficult concepts or ideas into focus. Have you ever heard the speeches of Martin Luther King Jr.? Decades after his passing, his words continue to move people. Then there are more current examples, such as Tony Robbins, Bob Proctor, or Brian Tracy. All of these individuals are amazing in their delivery of self-help information. Listen to their presentations and you can see how they really connect with their audiences.

Change requires communication, but change doesn't go over well if it is not communicated well. Every parent who communicates with a teenager can appreciate this point. Their child may not be able to articulate their frustration or the reasons behind it. An argument often becomes par for the course, leaving everyone frustrated and out of sorts. Misunderstandings can make change difficult to handle, because you may not understand why the change is occurring.

Companies often make this mistake as well. They may not clearly communicate their vision, so when they make changes, their employees are often left feeling frustrated and out of the loop. It can also make them feel uncertain about their job security, which can negatively impact their productivity. The reality is that miscommunication can have a large impact on whether change is welcomed or feared.

Communication is more than just speaking clearly. It is listening to and understanding the concerns of the other person and doing your best to address those concerns. When it comes to creating change in your life, you may find that you need to explain to your family why you are making that change. How do you communicate your choice? Often, how well it is communicated is reflected in the level of support you receive and if the change is embraced or not.

Have you been part of a change where the communication was less than you expected? How did that impact your ability to accept the change and create something incredible from that opportunity? For many of us, the answer is that the change was more difficult and we likely didn't support it wholeheartedly.

Again, the point is that communication can make a change easier to accept or a lack of it can make the implementation of a change more difficult. If you are initiating change in your own life, be sure that you are clearly communicating your needs to those around you. While they may not always agree with your decisions, they are much more likely to support them and the changes you want to make if you can clearly communicate the change and its impact.

Along with good communication, you need to be a good listener. Often misunderstandings occur because one individual is not really listening to the other. They may miss key instructions or details that could make the situation clearer. As a result, it can be easy to act without truly knowing all the necessary facts and circumstances. Can you see how not listening well could impact how you feel about a change in your life? It is also easy to see how others might be less supportive of change you initiate if they weren't listening.

How can you tell if someone is truly hearing you? Ask them questions and then clarify when it appears that they may not have gotten an accurate picture of what is about to occur. Some individuals may want to willfully misunderstand, and you want to do everything in your power to avoid that. At the same time, be a good listener. Don't listen to respond, but listen to understand their concerns, worries, and potential fears. Make adjustments to address their concerns where possible, but be as reassuring as you can when those adjustments might not be possible.

When you don't listen, you run the risk of missing key instructions or information that could directly impact your life or the change you are about to make.

I was always working, even from a young age. For a period of time, I worked on a gravel crusher as a ground person. My job was to go around and check for broken wheels, conveyors, and signs of wear and tear on other components. If something was wrong, I was to report it immediately to the tower person overseeing the operation. His job was to shut down the entire mechanical operation so the problem could be addressed. If he didn't, a major failure could occur, which could end up costing thousands of dollars of damage.

One morning, I was tired and didn't pay attention when I was relieving the previous shift. I had missed that a flashing was tearing and did not report it. An hour later, that flashing tore through. My boss saw it first. Gravel was everywhere. He had the operation stopped, then came over to the tool shack to fire me for not properly checking the system. That miscommunication cost the company time and money, plus I lost my job. The lesson? Communication and paying attention to the details is key to success in any area of your life, but especially when you are initiating major change.

Now let's talk about how a lack of communication can contribute to conflict. Our ability to connect with others can be hampered if we don't communicate well or if we are not sensitive to their needs and hot spots. Our personal and professional lives can be impacted by poor communication.

If you are considering acting to make changes in your life, start with how you communicate with others. We can all find areas to improve and make our connections with others deeper and more meaningful. The art of language is not easy. From birth, we are trained to communicate, but it doesn't come easily to all of us. Some become better than others at expressing themselves. The art of communication can be terrifying and amazing at the same time. You may also find it difficult to express yourself, especially when dealing with loved ones. How can you communicate more effectively with the individuals in your life?

Start by asking questions. This helps you gather information. Repeat back to the speaker your understanding of what they just said in response to your question. If they don't agree with your interpretation, keep asking for clarification until you get it. Be sure that you genuinely listen to the response before you start making assumptions. Try and imagine the situation from the other person's point of view. Be patient, because the best communication takes time.

There are also classes on public speaking and the art of communication. If you find yourself struggling consistently in this area, consider taking a course. The principles and real-world practice can help you improve your general communication skills. If you find yourself losing your train of thought, then consider writing down what you want to say. Be clear and concise where possible. Then use your written thoughts as a platform to bring up various points when appropriate within the context of the conversation.

Don't underestimate the power of practicing your communication skills in front of a mirror. This is where you can work on eye contact, exploring your various facial expressions, and also how to speak clearly. If you can talk to yourself, then it will get easier to talk to others. Make an effort to come out of your comfort zone, especially if you are not a good communicator. Consider it a change for the better.

Recognize that by improving your communication skills you can improve the quality of your life, as well as weather changing circumstances more effectively.

MOVE FORWARD WITH ME

Throughout this chapter, I have focused on some key areas that can make change more palatable, and reduce the fear and anxiety that commonly occurs. Still, the reality is that change, especially change we didn't initiate, can be overwhelming. Over the course of my lifetime, I have dealt with a variety of changes and I can say that not every experience was pleasant. But they all taught me valuable lessons.

I also want to remind you that change doesn't need to be something that occurs to you, but can be something you initiate. Consider areas of your life that are not as satisfying as you would like them to be. For example, are you struggling financially, but find yourself reluctant to make changes or take the risks necessary to turn your financial life around? Here is an area where making a change happen can have a significant impact.

However, don't limit yourself merely to material affluence. There are literally dozens of areas where you could find yourself hesitating to make changes. No matter what change you want to make, the mindset you choose will determine whether the change is successful or a struggle.

Throughout my work with individuals on changes in their lives, one thing has become clear; your mindset is key to making change work for you and allowing yourself to embrace change effectively.

I'm willing to work with you to help create the change that you want to see in your life. Let's face it, changes to our self-belief can lead to even more significant changes in other areas of our lives. With an improvement to your self-belief, there is no telling what you can accomplish. The changes to your point of view about yourself and what you can accomplish will help you make different choices about how you choose to live and work.

I believe that coaching is key to creating the right mindset to initiate and absorb changes in your life. A positive mindset allows you to see change in terms of what is possible, instead of focusing on the potential losses. Until you take the leap, you will never know exactly what is possible. But it can be hard to take those first steps to overhauling your thought process on your own.

I believe strongly in coaching and mentorship. It is a way to pass on the wisdom you have learned and the key strategies you may have discovered for addressing and initiating change. As part of my efforts to help others embrace change, my coaching and mentorship is available to you.

In my book, The Book of Change, I tackle a variety of topics and areas where you can start making small changes to build up to bigger ones. I also discuss how you can take dramatic and difficult circumstances and use them to learn and grow.

Using these tools, you can make a difference in your own life and in the lives of others. You can go from being fearful of change to being an example of embracing change for those in your family, your social circle, and your community. However, coaching isn't the only way to work on your skills to create and embrace change.

You can become a change advocate. That means allowing your positive mindset regarding change to influence others and impact their attitudes toward possible changes in their own lives. Your own example of dealing with change can serve as inspiration for others, which can then allow them to turn themselves into change advocates. It is a never ending cycle, which can give you peace of mind, even when faced with the toughest of challenges.

Additionally, there are other key takeaways for you to keep in mind as you start the journey to create change in your life. One way to embrace it is to understand what is happening and even to learn why.

Continuing education allows you to take the fear out of any change. After all, most of the fear of change stems from a lack of knowledge about what the change will mean for you, your family, and your community. When we are informed, change can be less intimidating, which can make us less fearful and more willing to take risks. Change is a part of taking risks to grow and explore our passions, achieve our goals, and fulfill our dreams. Without the right information and mindset, we will be unwilling to take the risks needed to achieve everything we imagine possible.

Clearly, you need to remember that change is a constant in your life. No one can escape it, no matter how risk adverse they may be. You need to embrace change for the benefits it can provide by creating a different mindset, gaining new skills, or even just acknowledging the personal growth that has resulted.

The change you see in your lifetime can and likely will have a profound impact on the lives of others, both now and in the future. Respect the people around you and demonstrate love and support when they are faced with changes, both large and small.

Contact me at **tony@tonydebogorski.com**. I would love to explore the ways that I can help you create real change in your life through adjustments to your mindset and increasing your willingness to learn and explore. Be inspired to create the meaningful life that you have always wanted and step away from living in fear of the unknown.

Amazing things are waiting for you! It is time for you to take the first step towards being a change agent in your own life.

Honor Your Inner Treasures

CELINA TIO

COLLECTIVE CREATED ME

"We are all created from our experiences, and the first step towards embracing our inner treasures is to acknowledge this. You are wonderful, and the experiences that took you to this point are all part of that. Do not be afraid of yourself; instead, let yourself shine." This quote is from my recent book, *Honor Your Inner Treasures*. It's an underlying principle of that work, and its message is most certainly applicable to what you're about to read in this chapter of *The Authorities*. Collective Created Me explains in the *Honor Your Inner Treasures* book, how most of our beliefs are obtained through training and repetition, and assumed personality through education. Becoming aware of the Collective Created Me is extremely beneficial because it puts you on the road to self-acceptance and realization, forgiveness, independence, appreciation and true happiness.

Think about this for a moment: do you remember someone in your family being sick when you were a child? Were the hours spent in family time talking about symptoms, where pain started, where it ended, how long it lasted, and medicines? It's likely that much of the conversation also revolved around nurses, doctors' assessments and trips to the hospital. Soon, with so much health and sickness related information taken in, you unconsciously started to become so familiar enough with that illness that you accepted it as just part of your family. It became so normal that you could quickly respond to questions about it as if it were your illness, too. "My uncle Charlie had it, and so did his son and my grandmother. It runs in our family."

Imagine if the conversation you heard about Uncle Charlie's illness had been about the way that healthy habits, physical activities, and letting go of toxic thoughts helped him recover. What would you have learned to do then in the event of an illness?

This example of negativity changing your perspective is applicable to other life experiences. What about love and relationships? Conversations about unfaithfulness, divorce, unhealthy relationships, abuse, violence? How has the negativity of those conversations affected your beliefs and the actions you've taken in life? Money is another example. People often say they never have enough money. Stories are shared about someone's new business failing, or friends who've lost their homes because they couldn't make their mortgage payments. Wouldn't stories of success have a more positive impact to encourage others to improve in their lives?

Most people receive diagnoses during their lives pertaining to health, personal finances, the country's economy, beauty, fashion and relationships. Usually, these diagnoses are fully accepted as truth and fact. There is an alternative, however. Why not see a diagnosis as feedback of that exact, precise moment and utilize it as the moment of opportunity to change, to create, to expand, to become, to discover, is opening up for you?

People often say when a door closes a window opens, and wait for the window to open right in front of them. Often, hoping that the window will magically pop open and the situation will change. The sad thing is, it may take a while and in the meantime the beliefs that life is not fair, life is hard or life is good to others start to run your thoughts.

I want you to know that all windows and doors are always open for you. Even more, there are no windows, there are no doors, because once you embrace your greatness you are free to live with purpose.

Going back to our example of listening to other people's life experiences, can you perceive how your fears and beliefs originated during these events? The occasions are wonderful moments to enjoy and remember the past, but sometimes people retell stories about illnesses with as much detail as they can recall. It's possible the now-adult children have no recollection of the event's seriousness because they remember with a child's naïveté only how happy they were about recovery. Now, listening to the story of an experience in your life that evoked sadness, these adults inevitably feel pulled down and relive that low-energy feeling. You can change that feeling in you and all the people around you. Next time you are at a reunion be sure to evoke moments that bring joy and laughter. Everyone will leave feeling great, having enjoyed the party, and with a more positive attitude for the next adventure in their life.

BECOME AWARE - CONNECT WITH YOUR INNER BEING

Let go of the stories and let go of others' experiences. Start living your own.

Embrace the belief that your life is complete and absolute just as is. Take a deep breath, aware of your body, starting at the top and working your way down. Begin with your scalp, your hair, your temples, your forehead, your eyebrows, your eyes, then move on until you reach the tip of your toes. It's important to take in every part of yourself so don't stop at the surface. Recognize your organs and their functions, even noting your breath as it travels into your lungs and fills you with pure oxygen. Become aware of your being. I ask that you become aware of your being, not that you look into the mirror or take a selfie and analyze it to see if you have wrinkles, or criticize your body shape. Stop judging yourself and start knowing yourself.

Selfies have become, to many, a tool to prove oneself, or a tool of confirmation of existence, presence and self-acceptance, and others' approval of the moment that is being lived.

As if the moment being lived needs external approval to be considered as a "perfect moment" and only then sharing it with the world.

When you look at the moment you are living as an image that "looks good" or "like happiness", the gap between what you are doing "looks great", and truly feeling great, is large. There is no enjoyment or happiness if it always depends on others' opinions. Making a picture look good when the emotions you are feeling at the moment don't match the illusion of the created image is keeping you from living a true honest happy moment.

Different from this is taking a picture to capture a moment of real pleasure and happiness, and the peace and joy that healthy relationships and celebrations bring. Those are photographs that recall true emotions of happiness, in turn aligning your whole being into feeling truly amazing. These selfies are not only a moment taken with a camera; they are taken into your soul, leaving a long-lasting impression in your life. Those are moments that you will truly love to share with others without deleting anything. What is your selfie telling you when you look at it? What is that image revealing?

Become aware of yourself and the moment without editing. Be completely honest about everything. In this moment of self-awareness, accept everything – your age, aches, sadness, longings, best memories, dreams – without shyness, even if they look too big at this moment. Become aware because for the first time in your life you will be truly, honestly and entirely present with yourself, as you know yourself to be at this moment. What is your inner self telling you? This is the true SELF you should be contemplating.

If you do this, for the first time in your life you will be truly, honestly and entirely present. Your unique, true self will be revealed. For many people, doing this will be the scariest meeting of their lives. To me it is the most amazing!

When working with my clients, this point of their journey is the most exciting to me. As their guide to reaching their true inner being throughout the Honor Your Inner Treasures™ Program, the transformation the client undergoes is magical, because their life suddenly expands as they embrace and accept fully their inner self.

YOUR EMOTIONS ARE POWERFUL. LEARN FROM THEM.

Pretending is the only sure thing someone does when they are denied their true feelings. Pretending to feel well, smiling just with the movement of the facial muscles, repeating clichés as a consolation to true feelings, and distancing ourselves from loved ones or hiding from life aren't effective measures. Not talking about problems doesn't solve them. On the contrary, the repetition of those actions and inner messages undoubtedly becomes the reality in your life, which extends the sadness, insecurity, lack of confidence, and low-energy life. It's an unhealthy cycle, difficult to break. Have you ever heard people complaining about the good luck of others, or blaming the sad circumstances in their life on other people's lives? If you come close to a person behaving this way, stay away. You don't want to adopt that attitude.

You can change, you can become more, and you can be the best amazing you because you truly, genuinely feel it. Sharing your life with others with honesty, because there is absolutely nothing to hide, is liberating. Accept that you are a human being experiencing life, and in the process are growing, becoming, expanding, and evolving.

Through this process there will be moments that call for change, whether of habits, beliefs, actions, or behaviors. Change is a process of evolving into a different state. The emotions that you carry through the transition are of most importance. Are you making the change out of resentment or fear? Is it happening because you don't feel you're enough? Or are you just resigning yourself because you are obedient to unhappiness. What if you make the change because you know that you would love and enjoy doing something different?

Ask yourself what you need to make this change? Maybe it's taking a course or learning something new. Going through training is a fun ride when all you are doing is acquiring new skills to master what you love to do! Don't let the fear of change keep you from becoming healthier and happier. You look and feel healthy and beautiful when you are enjoying the moments that you are creating in your life. Change gives you jolts of energy that propels you to do more.

CHANGE TO THE POSITIVE SIDE OF LIFE

"Change the thinking positive and acting negative attitude." – Celina Tio

I hear people talking about difficult situations in their lives that end with usual comments like "I'm staying positive," "I'm trying to think positive" or "Hopefully…" However, simply repeating the mantra "I'm staying positive" does not make it true. When you are vibrating in the true sense of positive energy your life has no room for negative energy. Positive will always see, hear, understand, interpret, and plan in a constructive manner. When clients come for their first consultations with me, I listen attentively to their voices. From their tones I can hear the negative energy of unhealed wounds, regardless of the words they use. They tell their stories as if they've become comfortable hurting. This is a common means of self-defense and emotional survival.

In their journeys through the Honor Your Inner Treasures™ Program, clients delve into their true selves and are guided through the process of transmuting their thoughts into a positive perspective. This transformation occurs once we do the necessary inner work at the soul level, which is the purest essence of being. Anger may become understanding and compassion; resentment an opportunity for self-reflection and inner growth; and solitude a time of self-forgiveness and self-acceptance. The more you discover about your inner being, the closer you are to the positive energy of your true self. Knowing that each step my clients take brings them closer to their inner being of positive creation gives me great joy. It is important to create life experiences in such a way that, when you reflect on the past, all you see is a magical garden of your own design that you can be proud of having imagined, lived, grown and created.

Let's do an exercise that will assist you with looking at decisions based on fear. You will need to sit comfortably on a chair and have with you a pad of paper and a pen. Imagine an "X" mark on the floor to your right that represents the change that you want to make, and an "X" to your left side. The "X" mark on the left side represents the negative reasons that you have to make the change in your life and the "X" on the right side represents positive ones.

On the paper write the reasons you want to make the change. For example, let's say that the decision you want to make is about a change in career. Write on the paper the thoughts that have crossed your mind. Use one piece of paper per thought about the issue. (It is important to follow these steps carefully.) Now, decide if the thought you've written is negative or positive and put the paper to your left or right side. Use the guide on the next page to help you determine whether your thoughts are positive or negative.

THOUGHT	LEFT SIDE	RIGHT SIDE
<u>I'm so fed up with my job.</u> I think I'll look for another one.	X	
<u>My job is so boring.</u> After doing the same thing every day for so long, it is not *exciting* anymore.	X	
I have been thinking of working part-time so I can go back to school. I'll have to cut down on expenses but I know it will be ok because I have some savings.		X
I have a job offer in another company <u>but</u> I would have to take a few courses to meet their requirement. a) I don't have the money to pay for the training b) It's hard to go back to class c) All your other "BUTS"	X	
<u>I hate going to work. The place is so toxic. The gossiping and competition is just sickening.</u>	X	

As you can see, on the column for thoughts I have underlined the negative comments. On the fourth example the word but is underlined because the "buts" are so big in our lives. You truly have to listen closely when you speak. Until you change your internal dialogue and are able to do this spontaneously, it is best to do this exercise by writing it on pieces of paper. Doing this will change the thinking positive and acting negative attitude that most people have without realizing why their lives are so difficult. Once you have identified your thought process about the issue, you can transform it and move all your thoughts to the positive side.

THOUGHT	LEFT SIDE	TRANSFORM & MOVE TO THE RIGHT SIDE
I'm so fed up with my job. I think I'll look for another one.	X	I'm more than ready to expand my possibilities. I know I have learned enough in my current position so I now realize I have room to grow.
My job is so boring. After doing the same thing every day for so long, it is not *exciting* anymore.	X	I love the feeling of excitement that bring new possibilities and learning new things. Change is great because I'm now ready.
I have been thinking of working part-time so I can go back to school. I'll have to cut down on expenses and [but] I know it will be ok because I have some savings.		This example shows how something that could be big "but I don't have money" is removed as an inconvenience and seen as something to work through.
I have a job offer in another company but I would have to take a few courses to meet their requirement. a) I don't have the money to pay for the training b) It's hard to go back to class c) All your other "BUTS"	X	This example is the opposite of the one above. Listen to all of your buts because they only pave the road ahead with more of the same in your life today. "No money" only brings you no money.
I hate going to work. The place is so toxic. The gossiping and competition is just sickening.	X	I have changed. I notice that my environment doesn't match the person that I am today. So it is time to move into a welcoming, healthy, prosperous, happy environment for me.

When you finish transforming your thought process, written now with only positive reasons, you will feel much more enthusiastic and energized to move forward and take the necessary steps to become or do. Every step of the way becomes more pleasurable because you have created a happy and positive future for yourself. What seemed to be big obstacles in the road are now the building stones and success is within reach! Congratulations! You truly do have the inner power to transform your life.

I have created a transformational workbook for my clients that enter the Honor Your Inner Treasures™ Program and as we go through the process they do simple, fun and motivating change processes. When they finish, only then the realization comes regarding how powerful it is to invest time into loving ourselves.

BELIEFS

All people have beliefs that help structure their lives. We know with great certainty that whatever we believe is true, and one of these beliefs is self-worth. People even determine their income based on their belief of self-worth. Your resume indicates exactly how much money you will make in the next year. When you review it and no changes have been made, you are hoping that inflation or the economy of the company you work for will determine the increase in the salary that you will be earning. Have you ever stopped to think about it? You are giving your power to another person to determine your growth, not only in your economy, but also your personal potential to do more, to become who you want to be.

I have worked with clients who are business owners feeling stressed out because of low funds, poor self-esteem and a lack of confidence. These issues not only impact their personal lives but also how their business grows. Those negative beliefs, ideas and limitations also have an impact on their earnings and the status of their finances, and all the people working for their company.

I remember working with Priti, a 43-year-old married woman. She emigrated to Canada from India, where she had received her degree as a software engineer. Once in Canada, Priti was able to obtain a position where

141

she could use some of her education and experience. The reason I say 'some' of her education and experience is because when she came to see me for the first time she said that she was starting to feel bored with her job and not living up to her full potential. Priti felt that there were problems in the company that took too long to solve and required great work to make operations run more efficiently. Doing things the way the company had done for years was causing the same problems over and over again. She wanted to make a change and had a vision to do so.

However, Priti was quiet and didn't like to be the center of attention, so she kept to herself, trying to fit into the company's mold. Eventually, the conflict between shyness and wanting to change operations caused her a great deal of stress. She could not feel confident putting forth her suggestions. And although there was nothing I could do to help her with her software issues, I was able to help her build her confidence to act, speak, think and move forward. With those new positive traits, she was able to increase her self-esteem and recognize her own value.

Being foreign and fearing she might appear ignorant to others was one of Priti's greatest stumbling blocks. To offset this, I offered a metaphor. I asked her to consider the plastic casing that envelops the computer containing the software she created. Is that foreign? Obviously, the answer is no. The casing is just another part of the whole computer just as she, too, is part of the whole.

In creation nothing is foreign. We are all co-creating contributing our energy into the amazing universe we all live in. This is why it is so important that you truly live your lives from your inner treasures because underneath your fears and doubts you are pure potential, everyone has amazing positive energy to add to the whole.

We also worked on Priti's self-esteem and confidence by training her subconscious mind to act, feel and think the way the leader she desired to be would. The leader she wanted to be was one who confidently and clearly communicated her views, ideas and solutions with the tone of a manager. In just a few weeks Priti noticed she was expressing her ideas, asking questions and sharing her knowledge and experience without feeling timid. Most importantly, she noticed that her peers welcomed her ideas.

Eventually, Priti realized this company didn't have potential to grow and she was putting all of her potential in a box too small for her. She knew she was ready to move on with confidence.

That spark of inner realization of your personal self, and of how truly valuable your contribution is to everything you do, changes everything. You become confident to plan and live your life making decisions that feel right, and feel an inner peace because you gained control. Now, you have the power to do the things that are truly important to you. Once you learn to expand your consciousness beyond your fear, the limitation you had becomes limit-less.

In my upcoming book, *Limitless Beliefs - 7 Steps to Transcend into a Joyful and Abundant You*, you will find the how-to for this process. To purchase, learn more about the book, www.limitlessbeliefs.com or www.celinatioauthor.com.

YOUR LIFE IS YOUR DECISION AND YOUR CREATION

"Create your life experiences in such a way that the day you look back all you see is a magical garden of your own design that you can be proud of having imagined, lived, grown and created." – Celina Tio

"Really? Are you sure? Because I was told…" These are all comments based on a lack of confidence. This does not have to be you! You are able to declare your independence, power and freedom! To embrace the true and pure intention of creation!

I'll share with you the experience of Laura, a beautiful and intelligent woman who came to my office for help. As she introduced herself and explained the reason why she had made the appointment, I was amazed. At 32 years old, she was a successful fashion designer. Her passion, however, was singing and songwriting. What an amazing girl, and what a disparity in her professional career compared to her dreams.

Her narrative was sad due to many of her life's circumstances and events. Her self-esteem and confidence was at an all-time low after ending a relationship that was going nowhere. Now, she hoped to let go of all her little self. Laura wanted to have more confidence to make decisions and communicate her ideas and feelings, and she wanted to feel good about herself. Simply put, she wanted to live happily.

I could have told her how beautiful, amazing and intelligent I thought she was. I could have pointed out all the wonderful opportunities she could have in life or how much I admired her. But she wasn't there for me to tell her what most any friend would. She needed to know from her own heart, discovering and loving herself so that she could go through her life's journey knowing her essence.

At the end of her journey I asked Laura to write what she decided was most valuable about herself. She took a few days and sent me an e-mail describing her value as she perceived it. Imagine the courage it took to be so vulnerable. Without relying on anyone else's opinions, she confessed her own beauty, strength, warmth and intelligence. She had honored her inner treasures.

I have asked her permission to share this with you because I want you to know that it is also possible for you. She kindly and happily agreed because she felt she could help other people. Maybe that person today is you or someone you love.

"I value myself because I am a strong person who perseveres through hardship, and I have faith I will get through it. I value myself because I am loving and kind-hearted person. I value myself because I take care of those in need and treat them just as I would treat myself. I value myself because I am a hard worker and very motivated. I value myself because I am a good woman. I value myself because I have self-respect and integrity, and will not allow anyone to take that away. I value myself because I am humble in life. I value myself because I am a good sister, friend, daughter, and lover because I care for people's feelings. I value myself because of my relationship with God and how I want to continue to help myself be better. I value myself because I am a loving woman who shares love with everyone. I value myself because I can make people laugh and really bring out the best in them; this shows me how amazing I am. I value myself because even if I am scared or fearful I have courage to face those fears. I value myself because of my ability to forgive and make amends even when people have truly hurt me. I value my positive thinking and my ability to turn what can be a bad situation into a great one. I value myself because I am able to express my feelings and my emotions now in a calm and mature way. I value myself because any goal I set for myself I achieve, because I am willing to work hard. I value myself because I always keep on smiling even when the going gets tough. I value myself because I am beautiful, strong, smart, mature, funny, loving, and kind person."

- Laura, Toronto, Canada
Fashion Designer/ Singer and Songwriter, naturally from the heart.

APPRECIATION

If life were a coin, would you say it is less valuable when you are looking on the head side just because the imprinted value is on the other side and you can't see it?

The value of everything is found through deep appreciation. Lots of people walk through life with the expectation of being accepted and liked by others, but they suffer a great deal when the world around them doesn't show them what they expect. Start increasing your self-value by appreciating your life as it is in this moment. Even if your world looks or feels different than you'd like, there is value to be found. You can increase that value by describing it and saying thank you. At first, it might take some creativity if you have been depreciating things most of your life.

Let's think of something you do every day, like eating. All of us eat when we are hungry, but some also eat when anxious, nervous or depressed. There is even a name for this: comfort food. Comfort food is supposed to make you feel better when you eat it; however, nobody has ever said, "I was feeling sad and I ate a whole bowl of ice cream and now everything is fine! All of a sudden I feel loved and my finances have improved drastically with every spoonful of food I ate!" This would simply not be true.

On the other hand, when you eat because you feel hungry your body and mind feel better because they receive the nourishment needed. If you offer and share your meal and spend time in the company of family or friends, your soul is nourished as well. In preparing your meal, be grateful that you have the ingredients on hand needed to prepare the meal that will nourish every cell in your body. Imagine all the minerals, vitamins, proteins, carbohydrates and fibers that are present in what you are about to consume, and how you are benefiting from them. Thank the supermarket for having them available for you, and the people who've dedicated their life into growing them. Even thank the work you do that earns you the funds to buy your food. It's crucial to become aware of the dimension of what you are about to eat.

- Be grateful to the soil that has the perfect nutrients to grow your food.

- Be grateful to the sun and the water for adding their energy.

- Be grateful to the universe for having created a planet that contains everything you need.

- Be grateful for the beauty of the colors, textures and aromas of the vegetables, herbs or fruits, or a cup of coffee.

- Be grateful to the person who will share this meal with you.

- Be grateful that you can share your moment with that person and have each other's company.

- Be grateful that you have the ability to offer and share your meal.

- Be grateful that life is allowing this moment to sit, rest, replenish, keep each other's company and share whatever it is that needs to be shared at the moment.

By now, appreciation has started to flow from the heart and you will know if what you are about to eat is healthy for you. If you have to thank the chemicals named on the package that are so difficult to pronounce instead of the natural sweet aroma of a natural ripe tomato, you will know not to eat it. Your body will show you resistance. When appreciation flows from the heart, you will feel true comfort even when you drink plain water. Do it at your next meal. Do the same with your home, your family, your pet and your neighbor. Practicing heartfelt appreciation will change your perspective on life.

SELF-REALIZATION

"You have the power of pure energy within you to be, to do, to have, to accomplish, to become your dream." – Celina Tio

When you truly know your essence, everything changes easily. Your relationships are healthier by helping you grow with people who share your life's path. Life becomes pleasurable and enjoyable, and conflict and stress no longer emanate from you. You understand that ego makes peoples lives sad and full of problems, and that it drives competition, fear, war and destruction.

Knowing your essence also means the things that you're doing now are in line with what makes you feel happy. It's easy to identify if you're off balance because life no longer feels whole. You become aware of your energy and how it affects everything around you. You have a fresh understanding that you are part of creation, co-creating with all that makes us one.

You become more independent when you know your essence, investing into your wellbeing and happiness instead of things that have no value to your personal self. Rich and wealthy has a whole different meaning now. No more spending to do things or obtain things just because you feel bored or empty. You'll no longer feel the need to shop in an attempt to feel happy or, even worse, to look happy. You become independent and know that you are the only one responsible for how you are living your life, with no one else to blame. Vacationing to escape from reality is a thing of the past. Instead, you'll have the freedom to choose a destination that will give you enjoyment in everything from the planning to the adventure to the return.

At this point, inner peace has become real in your life and you'll have the self-realization that you truly are the creator of every moment in your life. Your future is right this moment, so make it amazing and wonderful. Move from the comfort spot of sameness, obedience and unhappiness. Walking on your self-pity will take you only to more of the same. It is time to tell yourself that you deserve to experience life, and to savor and indulge in the sweetness and pure love of creation. You deserve to feel free of unnecessary pain, have inner peace and feel truly loved.

Of course we all have sad moments in our lives. It is normal to experience loss and birth, laughter with tears of joy and also tears of sadness, and expansion and contraction. It is the Yin and Yang of life. What's important is what you do with it.

Your inner being has been waiting for you to listen truthfully to the pureness within. You are powerful beyond your comprehension, and have more than strength. You have the power of pure energy within you to be, to do, to have, to accomplish, and to become your dream. When I realized how powerful I was created to be, I stopped feeling small. I rid myself of unnecessary fears, choosing instead to be one with the moment. I learned to breathe moments out of love, peace and joy, and to share it with you and everyone around me. Let me help you heal. Allow me to guide you into that place of discovering and once and for all Honor Your Inner Treasures. Your life will be transformed.

www.honoryourinnertreasures.com

www.limitlessbeliefs.com

www.celinatioauthor.com

The Pathway to Achieve Your Dream Life!

PHIL ARMSTRONG

This chapter will begin to illuminate your world in a way that will make lasting change possible. I want for you whatever big dreams you have, and I can certainly put you on the path to achieving them. But I also have a word of caution for you as you dream these big dreams: at some point you're going to begin to hear an inner voice say, "You can't do that!" Well, I say to you ignore that voice, because he is a liar. He represents a part of you that wants comfort not change, relaxation not tireless pursuit, and certainty instead of self-confidence. This is your worst enemy.

So, first and foremost, you must identify and get passed the liar in your head. To do this, you'll have to learn to listen for the voice and then practice not taking its advice. Also, learn to distinguish between the negative and the positive voices in your head (yes, there's more than one voice!). It may seem difficult at first, but I have every reason to believe whatever your mind can conceive—along with Desire, Faith, Focus, Determination, and Action—your mind can achieve.

DESIRE

Desire is the starting point of all achievement. To create or cultivate desire, you must know what it is you want from life—the type of lifestyle, the kind of relationships, even the amount of money you want to earn and keep. Specifically, you need to sit down with paper and pen and define the things you want. Once you have created both a physical and a mental picture of them, then you can think about setting some goals to achieve them.

So, let me get you started. Take time now to answer the questions below. They're meant to help you get a better glimpse of your purpose and create some desire to take action.

1. What makes you smile?

2. What are your favorite things to do?

3. What activities make you lose track of time?

4. What makes you feel great about yourself?

5. Who inspires you most?

6. What are you naturally good at?

7. What do others ask for your help with?

8. If you had to teach, what would you teach?

Note: for a complete list pick up my book, "The Keys to Think and Grow Rich," set up a coaching session or ask about one of my seminars in your area. I can be reached at armstrongbreakthrough.com.

In addition to the desire to take action, you really do need to put good thoughts into your head instead of lousy ones. Why? Because you need to be in a good place to conquer the list of the top reasons people fail. Some of these include:

1. Lack of well-defined purpose in life

2. Lack of ambition to aim above mediocrity

3. Insufficient education

4. Lack of self-discipline

5. Ill health

6. Procrastination

7. Lack of persistence

8. Negative personality

As you go over this list, study yourself to discover how many of these causes of failure stand between you and success.

For a full list pick up my book, set up a coaching session, or ask about one of my seminars in your area. Go to armstrongbreakthrough.com.

Next, I want you to ask yourself this question: are you just interested in achieving your dreams and desires, or are you committed to achieving them?

Those who are just interested will do what's easy, and what everybody else does, while the committed ones will do what it takes—they'll practice, study and put in the effort to persevere until their desires are achieved. They won't make excuses, they'll stop blaming and they'll give up their victim stories. Instead, they'll focus on how they can achieve their goals.

The way to achieve your goals is to:

1. Fix in your mind exactly what it is that you desire. Write it down.

2. Determine exactly what you intend to give in return for what you want. Write it down.

3. Establish a definite date when you intend to acquire what you want. Write it down.

4. Create a definite plan for carrying out your desire. Write it down.

5. Begin to put your plan into action, whether you're ready or not.

6. For each goal you're working on, read your written statements out loud, twice-daily—once just before retiring at night and once after rising in the morning.

Note: repeat the process for each specific goal you have (by writing out a clear, concise statement of the goal you intend to achieve, naming the time limit for its achievement, stating what you intend to give in return for it and describing clearly the plan through which you intend to achieve it).

As you read, see and believe yourself already in possession of what it is that you want.

In my book, "The Keys to Think and Grow Rich," I talk about the Four Pillars of Goal Setting: Financial, Health & Fitness, Relationships & Spiritual, and Legacy & Charity. Pick up a copy, set up a coaching session, or enquire about our seminar package. You can do this at armstrongbreakthrough.com.

FAITH

Is all it takes to achieve your dreams desire and a bunch of well-defined goals? Not a chance. You'll need faith.

Faith is a state of mind—an active state of mind—in which the mind is in the process of relating itself to the great vital force of the universe. The best way faith can be explained is to say that it's—humanity's awareness of, belief in and harmonizing with the universal power surrounding him. Faith establishes a working association with the power variously referred to as the Universal Mind, the Divine Mind, and by religionists, as God.

Faith may be induced, or accessed, by affirmation or repeated instructions to the Subconscious Mind through the principle of auto-suggestion. Repetition of orders given to your Subconscious Mind is the only known method of voluntary development of the emotion of faith. All thoughts that have been emotionalized (given feeling), and mixed wth faith, begin immediately to translate themselves into their physical equivalent or counterpart. The emotions, or the feeling portion of thoughts, are the factors that give faith, vitality, life and action.

Please note that the Subconscious Mind does not discriminate between constructive thoughts or negative thoughts, and will work with the material we feed it. Through our thought impulses, the Subconscious Mind will translate into reality a thought driven by fear just as readily as it will translate into reality as a thought driven by courage or faith.

Your belief, or your faith, is the element that determines the action of your Subconscious Mind.

There's nothing to hinder you from deceiving your Subconscious Mind when giving it instructions through auto-suggestion. To make this deceit more realistic, conduct yourself as you would if you were already in possession of what you're suggesting to your mind. One believes whatever one repeats to oneself. Every man is what he is because of the dominating thoughts that he permits to occupy his mind. Repeat a lie enough times and you will begin to believe it is true.

To help you get a better understanding of how the mind works to bring into your life the people, the places and the things that you need to build your dreams, consider the following stories.

THE PLACEBO EFFECT

A recent Baylor College of Medicine study on the outcome of arthroscopic knee surgery demonstrates the placebo effect. A group of patients with painful and worn-out knee joints were given two types of surgery: one group had the actual surgery, and the other was just given a surgical scar. Two years later, patients reported equal improvement in pain relief and knee function. There are thousands of studies such as this, showing the placebo medication or surgery was as effective as the real thing. Why? The Subconscious Mind was told that it would work, and it expected to do just that! Remember, the Subconscious Mind cannot tell the difference between the real and the imaginary.

TUG MCGRAW— YOU GOTTA BELIEVE!

Few people know that when Phillies pitcher Tug McGraw struck out batter Willie Wilson, in the bottom of the ninth to win the 1980 World Series, the game played out exactly as Tug planned it. When interviewed and asked how he felt at that tense moment, Tug surprised them when he said, "It was as if I'd been there a thousand times before. When I was growing up, I would pitch to my father in the backyard. It would always get to the place where it was the bottom of the ninth, three men on, and two outs. I would bear down and strike out that last man to win the World Series." Because Tug conditioned his mind, day after day, in the backyard, the day eventually arrived where he was living out that dream for real.

The previous story reminds me to tell you a little about The Law of Attraction. When I think of faith I often use this law. It states that if you put yourself out into the universe, then whatever it is you desire will begin to move toward you. The stronger your faith, the stronger the attraction. Learn more about this law by picking up my book, "The Keys to Think and Grow Rich," setting up a coaching session, or asking about one of my seminars in your area. I can be reached at armstrongbreakthrough.com.

FOCUS

What can I say about the power of adding focus to your life? People like Earl Nightingale, Maxwell Maltz and Napoleon Hill became famous for their discoveries of the importance of focusing your thoughts on the positive; on those things you want in your life. Conversely, they understood the opposite was also true: you must guard against thoughts other than those you want in your life. In fact, they had in their hands the very cure to the ills of this world—

looking to the light rather than to the dark, zooming in on the positive rather than entertaining the negative, saying yes to life rather than saying no.

But if it really is that simple, then why isn't everyone healthy, wealthy and happy? It goes back to my earlier comments regarding the way the Subconscious Mind works. The subconscious can't tell real from imagined, and it has no filter other than the choices you make; the thoughts you choose to focus on are what it has to work with. You can make this process easier by internalizing these thoughts with strong emotion, dialing up the focus, so to speak. It's here where most people get in trouble.

Nobody in school ever taught you that your Subconscious Mind is what will bring the world to your doorstep. No one ever told you to ay attention to the conversation in your head, because your subconscious is listening too. The average person thinks tens of thousands of thoughts every day and is only aware of a small fraction of them. Of those thoughts they are aware of, very few are placed there "on purpose" and with forethought as to what they want those thoughts to do. Finally, average people definitely don't know how to best focus those thoughts for winning results.

Affirmations, written or oral statements that confirm something is true, are the missing key. The person who stands before the mirror and says with conviction, "I will earn an extra thousand this month." may feel silly, especially when he or she says it ten times in a row morning and night. But that person (you) is focusing those thoughts. When you use affirmations, you are painting a bullseye on your Subconscious Mind (or Spirit). Remember, the subconscious can't tell real from imagined. It will, instead, get to work on making that affirmation happen for you.

Furthermore, thoughts you continuously impress upon your Subconscious

Mind over and over become fixed in that part your personality. Fixed ideas will then continue to express themselves without any conscious assistance until they are replaced, something we refer to as a habit.

All this may sound a bit out there, but it has been proven to work. The body is the material presentation of you. It's an instrument of the mind. Your thoughts are impressed upon the Subconscious Mind which moves your body into action, which produces your results. Your Conscious Mind thinks, your Subconscious Mind feels and your Body produces action, which determines your results.

$$\text{Thought} + \text{Emotion} = \text{Action}$$

DETERMINATION

Determination when pursuing big dreams is all about being resolved to do the things you must do in order to achieve those dreams. It's about replacing thoughts of doubt with positive thoughts that elicit useful emotions, especially when facing obstacles that appear to be insurmountable.

Again, we come back to the two mind theory: the Conscious Mind, which reasons, and the Subconscious Mind, which feels. Put the two of them together, working in unison, and you get strong action as a result.

But let's consider this in reverse. What's happening when emotions bubble up from the subconscious unsummoned (these could be positive or negative in nature)? A habit has been triggered. A habit you may not even be aware exists. A habit that can, and will, threaten your determination to carry out your action steps or goals. How? If the triggered emotion is strong enough and the action it tends to bring about is one you resort to a lot, then you could find yourself taking actions completely opposite to the ones you need to be taking.

Such habits have probably been created without you ever being aware of what was happening. This is why it's important to pay attention (at least in situations involving your dreams and goals) to your self-talk. You see, the thoughts—and the emotions they evoke—are the result of your two minds communicating with each other, and they can give you a pretty clear picture of what's going on.

So, if you discover that your self-talk isn't helping you at the moment, I want you to remember that you have the freedom of choice to change it (by using affirmations). Don't make the mistake of thinking that you are locked into a certain way of thinking or feeling. It simply takes a little longer to communicate with your Subconscious or Spirit Mind than it does with your Conscious Mind. Let me give you an example.

Penny is feeling dejected this morning. She can't seem to get motivated. There's a presentation on her desk for a client she's meeting at 1 p.m. and all Penny can think about is going for a walk in the park. She remembers a seminar she went to that taught people how to change their thoughts and emotions into more useful ones. Penny writes some sentences on a piece of paper, and then grabs her purse and heads to the washroom.

Standing in front of the washroom mirror, Penny recites what she has written down, 10 times for each sentence.

- Winston (her client) trusts me.

- This solution will work for him.

- The sale is guaranteed!

Penny then rubs her hands together quickly for a few seconds before clapping them together and saying "Yes!" in an excited voice. A thrill of emotion runs through her and she's suddenly energized (like she was in the seminar where she learned to do this). Her thoughts immediately turn to her presentation, so she returns to her desk and goes back to work.

To learn more please contact me at armstrongbreakthrough.com.

ACTION

As you can see, getting results is all about motivating yourself (specifically your body) to take pre-planned actions specifically designed to produce said results. Notice I said "pre-planned actions." Motivation for those actions depends on how the Conscious and Subconscious Minds interact. So, writing down your goals forces you to think those exact words. Doing affirmations further instructs the mind and brings emotion and your subconscious into play, which is where your motivation to act will come from. Usually, the greater the emotion, the greater the motivation to act.

People will look at you funny if you tell them you are pre-planning your actions for tomorrow, but I find it strange that anyone would choose any other way of going through life than "on purpose." Think about it. Most people go through their days buffeted by the winds of life. They don't live "on purpose," and that's a shame. We have free will for a reason. You get to choose what you do and what things mean to you every single second of every day.

Think about that for a few minutes! You can actually decide what anything means. A death can be a blessing. Or it can be sad. It can also be a reason to celebrate the person's life. Your past, something the average person drags along into the future with them, doesn't have to have any meaning at all. It's just a bunch of things that happened to you. You are free to just BE IN THE MOMENT, open to all the possibilities of the future and ready to spring into action with your dreams and goals firmly in mind. There's another way of saying all this …

Every January over 65 % of Americans make new year's resolutions, and 92 % of these people never achieve them. A Harvard MBA study showed that 3 % had written goals and plans, and 13 % had goals but only in their mind, while the remaining 84 % had no goals. 10 years later it was found that the 13 % earned twice as much as the 84 % and the 3 % earned 10 times as much as the 97 percent combined.

In his best seller book, "Think and Grow Rich," Napoleon Hill states that setting goals and plans to achieve them is the starting point of all achievement. I can't think of a better reason for being "on purpose" in this life.

One little reminder: when you take pre-planned action, make sure it covers every base and then some. In other words, take MASSIVE ACTION!

Want to learn more? Send me an email at armstrongbreakthrough.com

THE UNIVERSAL ALL

The Universal All is something I came up with to discuss the one aspect of achievement that we haven't yet visited. There are thousands of other names for this power but rather than just define the name, I want to define the activity. You see, for three thousand years all the great thinkers have all agreed upon one point—that there is a power, and this power creates, animates and motivates the entire cosmos.

How does this power animate and motivate? What are some of its distinguishing features? To determine the answer to my question we will first refer to the school of science and the school of theology.

Science, the study of knowledge, calls it "Energy."

What is energy? They say it just is!

It's neither created nor destroyed.

It's the cause and effect of itself.

It's 100% present in all places at all times.

What does theology say this power is?

They say it is "God."

Describe God. He just is.

He's neither created nor destroyed.

He's the cause and effect of himself.

He's 100% in all places at all times.

Wernher von Braun, father of the space program, stated that "science studies this force that surrounds humanity and theology studies this force that is within humanity. Someday they will agree that they are studying the same thing."

I believe that to gain the good life we all desire so much, we must understand how to relate to this great power. We don't necessarily have to understand it— that's the faith part of things— but we do need to know that we're part of it. Just remember, theology studies the spirit, while science studies the physical.

When we say we are burned out, we are referring to both energy (the physical) and emotions (the spiritual). When we say we are motivated, we are also saying we are energized. When we act, we can feel both the physical and the emotional components of that state.

So, if I can use my conscious mind, which is more a part of the physical world, to energize my subconscious or spirit mind, then it begs the question—are these things not related? Is it possible that they may even be the same thing? And if they are, how can we use this knowledge?

In real life, there appears to be a veil between the physical and the spiritual. As we attempt to communicate across that veil it seems that we need to purposefully place our communications into the physical or conscious mind. We can do this best by sight. We write things down and look at them, placing them firmly into our mind as bold thoughts. Then we must purposefully place our communications into the Spirit or Subconscious Mind. We do this vocally and with emotions. We feel what we want as we say what we want. The result is some level of action being asked of our bodies. We're summoned. The higher the energy and the higher the emotion we achieve, the greater the action of which we are capable becomes. Interesting stuff.

SUMMARY

Whatever your mind can conceive of your mind can also achieve. This is a fundamental truth, but there is a part of you that I refer to as the liar. Its voice will appear in your head as you progress through ever more challenging goals. This part of you wants comfort not change, relaxation not tireless pursuit, and certainty instead of self-confidence. Luckily, you also have a positive voice—a helper—that will allow you to counter the effects of the liar's voice on your psyche. Unless you have a very good reason to do otherwise, listen to your helper and ignore the liar. Once passed the liar, achievement is a matter of following a prescribed set of steps. These include: desire, faith, focus, determination, and action.

DESIRE: It's easier to dream big, and to create both a mental and written picture of these things, if you create a list of things you love to do that will solve problems for the people who surround you. It's better than the alternative of continuing to follow rules that just don't work. Think about this as you progress from dreams to concrete goals and action steps. We also reviewed a partial list of common causes of failure.

The way to achieve your goals is to write out a clear, concise statement of each goal you intend to attain, name the time limit for its attainment, state what you intend to give in return for it and describe clearly the plan through which you intend to achieve it. Read your written statements out loud, twice-daily: once just before retiring at night and once after rising in the morning.

FAITH: Your mind is driven by thoughts; your body is driven by emotion. Faith is an emotion. It's something that happens when we try to connect to the universe around us. Wrap specific thoughts or calls to action in the emotion of faith—through written and spoken affirmations—and your Subconscious Mind will go to work on the problem. This will usually put your body to work on the problem (motivation). Note: the Subconscious Mind can't tell the difference a between real or imagined experience. This means you can manipulate it to do your bidding.

FOCUS: Thought + Emotion = Action. You can extrapolate that if certain thoughts and emotions are focused on the Subconscious Mind, then your motivation will be dialed up as well. This happens to be true. You just have to make your affirmations as convincing as possible. Also, the more you repeat your affirmations, the greater and more focused the actions you are eliciting become, until what you've been after becomes a habit you don't have to think about anymore.

DETERMINATION: It's all about being resolved to do a thing, to choose to bring to bear both the Conscious Mind (reason and thought) and the Subconscious Mind (emotions), until you are motivated to take massive action with respect to solving one of your goals. The tool you use for this is affirmations.

ACTION: You can decide how you're going to act in advance by using affirmation to create a habit. One thing that arises from this truth is that you don't have to act in certain ways in a given situation. The corollary is that you decide what things mean. Decide what things mean to you—in any given moment—and it results in personal freedom; the freedom to be in the moment, to do anything, to BE anything, to choose from all the possibilities of the future that lies before you.

THE UNIVERSAL ALL: For three thousand years all the great thinkers have all agreed upon one point—that there is a power, and this power creates, animates and motivates the entire cosmos, including you. Scientists call it Energy, religionists call it God. What you call it may not matter because IT is in you. The subconscious represents the physical and the subconscious represents the emotional. What if they are the same thing in different forms?

Enter Into a Passionate Relationship with Your Own Life

SILVANA AVRAM

Have you ever wondered whether there is more to life than meets the eye? Do you feel that despite all your achievements true fulfilment still eludes you?

Join me on this transformational journey where you will learn to see yourself and your life in a different light.

- You will find out how to ask the right questions.

- You will learn to identify the main reason why you find yourself trapped in the same vicious circle.

- You will redefine the true meaning of being and uncover the source of deep fulfilment.

- You will be able to decide whether you are ready to embark on the journey to personal fulfilment.

My passionate plea to you is to allow this introduction to the secret of lasting fulfilment to work as a powerful catalyst for you. Should you want to explore the topics addressed here in more depth I invite you to read my book "Being You And Loving You – The Ultimate Guide To Fulfilment" – where I guide you through twelve life changing steps to true fulfilment. Together with the book you will also find plenty of free materials, insights and support at www.BeingYouAndLovingYou.com

It is the aim of this chapter to empower you to start your journey to true fulfilment. Are you ready? Let's dive in!

YOUR JOURNEY TO FULFILMENT STARTS WITH ASKING THE RIGHT QUESTIONS

"The Universe contains three things that cannot be destroyed;
Being, Awareness and LOVE"

— *Deepak Chopra*

"What is the meaning of life?" Human beings have searched for an answer to this question for millennia. Sages, philosophers, religious figures and scientists have all put forward their hypotheses, and each interpretation added yet another nuance to a mystery that remains as fascinating and as alluring as it has always been.

So: "Why are we here?" And why is it that this most important question of all is also one of the most avoided? Perhaps we have long accepted that there is no answer to it. Perhaps facing this question feels so…unsettling that we prefer to bury it under more…urgent matters. Like finding a job and paying the next bill.

168

I put to you another possibility. I believe that "Why are we here?" is indeed an unanswerable question. At least for the time being. And so is *"What is the meaning of life?"*

Why? Because they are too vast...and too vague!

Does that mean I am advising you to drop the questioning altogether and simply get on with your life? No, not at all! Not if you want to live a joyous, meaningful life. Not if you are looking for true fulfilment. In fact, if this is what you are after, it is vitally important to keep questioning.

But you must learn to ask the right questions.

I believe that each one of us must start with the more manageable "Why *am I* here?" or "What is the meaning of *my* life?"

I believe that each one of us must take responsibility for our own answers.

You see, when you allow someone else to answer these questions for you, you give away your power (and with that your responsibility). You may like a particular answer/ philosophy for a while and you may find it resonates with you – you may even dedicate your life to promoting it – but it will still not be yours – and as such it will not fully transform your life, it will not bring you the fulfilment you crave. You may read as many books as you want and you may attend endless wonderful seminars...They will all help you feel good for a while and you are sure to get some valuable insight. But no person and no book can truly change your life for you. Only when you find the strength and the courage to stay with the question of meaning long enough to allow for your own answer to be born in you, will you find the infinite joy and freedom that come from knowing. It is only *your own* answer that will truly transform *your life*. It is owning that answer that brings true fulfilment.

If your life is a riddle, the only way to fully - fill it… is to find your own answer to it.

Now that you know where to start…how do you actually do it?

You can find your own answer by asking the right questions, either on your own or by engaging in a philosophical dialogue with friends and other people interested in the same quest for meaning. You must be patient and tenacious, and not give up at the first signs of exhaustion or disappointment. After all, the question of meaning is the most challenging question of all, and many choose to avoid it altogether. But if you stay with it, if you make it an intrinsic part of your journey, sooner or later you will be rewarded.

You will not be alone in your endeavour. One of the most famous of the Delphic maxims inscribed in the pronaos (forecourt) of the Temple of Apollo at Delphi, Ancient Greece, and quoted by many, most famously by Socrates as the main character in Plato's dialogues, was *"Know Thyself"*. Through the ages there have been many who have embarked on this arduous journey.

Today, there is a modern variant of the life-transforming dialogues left to posterity by Plato: the coaching dialogue. The Philosopher is replaced by the more modest Coach. They are similar, however, in that the Coach, like the Greek philosopher but unlike a religious figure or a mentor, is not providing the answers. Instead, she or he is merely providing you with the right questions, gently challenging you when you go off track and often holding a symbolic mirror in which you start to see your true reflection and find your own answers.

It is a true measure of our 21st Century's *Age of Knowledge* that Coaching has become such an accessible experience. Perhaps this is a sign that more and more amongst us are ready and willing to stay with the question of meaning and find the true purpose of our lives. Perhaps more and more people are ready to embark on the journey to true fulfilment. Are you?

BEING SUCCESSFUL IS NOT THE SAME AS SUCCEEDING AT BEING

"What makes you think human beings are sentient and aware? There's no evidence for it. Human beings never think for themselves, they find it too uncomfortable. For the most part, members of our species simply repeat what they are told – and become upset if they are exposed to any different view. The characteristic human trait is not awareness but conformity.."

— Michael Crichton

"I am a human being, not a human doing. Don't equate your self-worth with how well you do things in life. You aren't what you do. If you are what you do, then when you don't...you aren't."

— Dr. Wayne Dyer

Before we proceed to consider what your journey to true fulfilment might look like when you embark on a path of enquiry and examination, I would like you to briefly stop and take a look at your life right now.

Do you love your life? Do you love yourself? Do you feel deep gratitude and awe about who you are? Do you feel blissful, fulfilled and radiant, sharing your wisdom and your light with everyone else, in compassion?

Chances are that you don't.

Chances are that you don't even believe this is possible!!

But if it were possible, would you like to feel like this? Would you like to live your life with absolute joy, and share your happiness with others?

I hope your answer to that last question is yes.

If it is, you have already taken the first step to fulfilment.

You see, most people have already given up on personal fulfilment. Most people have somehow fallen into the trap of believing that there is nothing more to life than work, duty, supporting family and friends, and the occasional recreation. It may sound incredible, but most people have convinced themselves that life is more about sacrifice and suffering than about being happy. If asked, of course everyone would say they want to be happy. Yet most people spend their lives doing things that take them farther and farther away from being joyful and fulfilled.

Most people spend most of their lives *doing* things. In fact doing so many things that they don't have the time to stop and ask *why* they are doing them.

Most people spend their lives doing so many things that they forget to Be.

But how can I forget to be? I hear you ask.

What else is there to 'being' that I haven't got already? Is it not enough that I am…alive? How can I be …being? How can I Be more?

You see…rocks and trees and animals are too. They exist. Life flows through them and expresses through them without encountering much opposition. They are pure expressions of life.

And so are we. Except for the fact that we also have the wonderful gifts of thought, of mind…of consciousness.

I want you to consider that maybe, just maybe, for us humans it is not enough to be alive, to truly Be. If it were, we would all be happy – or at least at ease. We would not ask questions. We would not search for more.

What makes us different is that we have the gift of being able to be aware

172

of being. It is this gift, and whether or not we choose to use it, that makes all the difference.

In order to truly Be as a human being you must be aware of who you are – of your potential. You must get involved in "being", become responsible for your "being", become the co-creator of your life.

When, on the other hand, we choose not to use the gift of awareness, we spend most of our lives doing things, being alive without truly being aware of the mystery, the complexity and the beauty of our being. We allow doing to take over, we throw ourselves into doing with a vengeance, seeking solace in temporary achievements that often leave us emptier than before.

Why and how does this happen? When we live without fully being present to our own lives, to our own being, we function on automatic pilot much of the time. Most of the functions we perform require so little of our conscious input that we get used to being disengaged. It's easier. We do the minimum and we get by. If we are "lucky" we can spend our whole life without having to account for the huge lack of …presence in it. For the most part, everyone is doing the same, and we are covered. No one will know. No one will dare ask.

But is that truly "lucky"? Is our life really about "getting by"?

If it were, mere survival would qualify as fulfilment. You would already and at all times feel fulfilled. Yet most of us know deep down inside our hearts that our lives must be more than just survival.

Perhaps our life is about success?

The difference between success and fulfilment is that success, as it tends to be defined, is still at the level of doing. You can become successful by following instructions and still staying on autopilot. In fact, the more autopilot-friendly the system you follow, the more successful you probably are in that particular area.

It is a common mistake to equate success with fulfilment. Many people who do, realize that success has not brought them the fulfilment they wished for. Many of these people spend years wondering where they went wrong and what's missing.

Our society seems to conspire to push us towards a narrowly defined form of success that rarely allows any space for true fulfilment. In other words, our misinterpretations are not entirely our fault. We are taught from early on to play by the (widely accepted) rules. We trust our parents and our teachers, and we unwittingly follow in their footsteps. We keep ourselves busy doing so many things that we have little time for self-exploration or personal inquiry, for Being. It is this restless drive for doing more and more that slowly but surely derails us from the only achievement that matters: understanding, accepting and expressing – in fact Being - our true self. Unless we stop to ask the right questions we don't even realise what we are missing.

To sum it up, success in doing cannot lead to fulfilment, for the simple reason that it involves operating at a different level.

To achieve true fulfilment you must operate at the level of Being.

It is not being successful at doing that will make you feel fulfilled.

To be fulfilled you must succeed at Being.

* * * *

So far we have learnt that in order to be fulfilled you must start by asking the right questions: "What is the meaning of my life?" "Why am I here?"

Tackling these and similar questions of meaning helps you become aware: aware that there is more to life than meets the eye; aware that as a human being it is not enough to be alive…Nor is it enough to be doing many things.

We then looked at what happens when you don't ask these questions. When you avoid questioning the true meaning of your life you get sucked into a life of endless doing with very little time for Being – and hence, with very little or no chance of feeling fulfilled.

For most people the question of meaning is an intimidating one, and one they'd rather put aside. After all, why take responsibility for one's life when it seems easier to just get by? Many people "succeed" in avoiding this question altogether. They also miss the opportunity of living deeply fulfilling, joyful lives. For others, something happens that forces them to wake up to it. It could be an unexpected turn of fate, a tragic event, even a major bonus, like winning the lottery, that pushes them to take a deeper look in the mirror. At those times they discover that there is a whole new dimension to 'being' that they were completely ignoring before. It is then up to them to embark on a journey of discovery that should ultimately lead them to true fulfilment.

There is, of course, a more natural, organic way that comes when you simply decide to take responsibility for your life and actively explore the gifts it promises to offer. You do it because you realize this is the only way you are going to feel truly happy and fulfilled. You do it because you want to be a co –creator in your life and express your full potential.

Along the way you may need the help of a friend, a sage or a coach – and you may be able to help others – but ultimately each one of us must find our own answers in order to express the true richness of our lives.

Once you are on the path to fulfilment there is no going back. You taste the ecstasy of being alive. Everything thereafter is a miraculous discovery, a wonderful adventure, a self-affirming deed and a deeply fulfilling expression of who you are. You have been kissed by life.

TRUE FULFILMENT COMES FROM AN AUTHENTIC AND LOVING RELATIONSHIP WITH YOUR LIFE

"The first step toward change is awareness. The second step is acceptance."

— *Nathaniel Branden*

We have established that in order to find true fulfilment you must be able to start with the right question and you must be able and willing to stay with it until you find your own answer. This is no easy journey. But it is the only one that will get you to true fulfilment. And as such, it is the most exciting journey of all.

If you are looking for deeper fulfilment, if you have started to realise that fulfilment will not come from doing more "stuff", chances are that you are already awakening to the possibility of an infinitely richer you. It does not matter how long it took you to get to this point. What matters is that you are ready: ready to embark on the beautiful, empowering, liberating and ultimately fulfilling journey of Being; ready to Be. Now.

Congratulations! Let the journey begin!

＊ ＊ ＊ ＊

As a coach, I can never get tired of seeing my clients find true joy and meaning in their lives. It often feels as if I watch them learn how to fly. And when they take off on their own…The sense of unlimited potential, freedom and happiness that comes with finding your own answer to the mystery of life is truly indescribable. One must experience it to be able to understand it.

But, if you will allow me, I would like to share with you what you might expect along the way.

There are two essential ingredients that will ensure a successful journey.

1. In order to be fulfilled you must first learn to Be.

2. Then you must learn how to Love Being.

As we touched upon earlier, truly Being requires presence and awareness.

True fulfilment comes when you and your life become one. When you live passionately...fully. To be one with life you must first wake up to Being; you must be aware of who you really are.

To start with, this will involve exploring your strengths, your talents, your gifts. It will mean looking at what makes you *you*, what makes you unique. In case you are already backing off in fear, rest assured. Every one of us is unique. Your special features, your memories and stories, your thoughts and feelings, your desires and dreams...all these make you a world unto itself, a uniquely beautiful expression of life, an exquisite original work of art in constant motion. There is no one else in the entire universe like you. There has never been and there will never be! You just have to muster the courage to embrace this truth! And allow it to transform you! It will help to have someone else hold the mirror, but once you learn to look at yourself in this way you will be able to see your life in a different light.

(To learn more about how you can embrace and celebrate your uniqueness visit www.SilvanaAvram.com)

It will then be important to find ways to truly express who you are; to listen to your heart and let it teach you everything you had tried to forget. Becoming aware of your thought patterns and connecting with your deepest emotions will enable you to re-define yourself. Then you can move one step further and try your hand at re-creating who you are. Being you is the gift you were given. Accepting this gift and then bettering it will be the gift you give back to life. How wonderful. This is pure creation. It's a miraculous process. Let it be fun!

At this point you should be ready to start thinking of how you could share your gift with others. This will become your purpose. That's when the real magic begins. And with it, true joy.

This is the point on your journey when your love relationship with life truly begins. The intimate loving relationship that you have managed to build with yourself expands into a passionate love affair with your life.

Now that you have become the co-creator of your life you must allow yourself to fall in love with your creation. You and your life must become one. This means moving from living your life into allowing your life to live, to express through you. You must be in awe of your life, you must respect it and cherish it and place it above anything else. Because your life is your gift to yourself and to the world. Because your life is the most intimate expression of who you are.

Loving your life is acknowledging and loving the infinite potential that you are. Loving your life with passion will teach you how to love every life with passion – will help you connect with every other life in compassion and joy. Knowing that you have expressed the best of you gives you the licence to feel free, to feel happy, to feel fulfilled.

When you live your life with this intensity there is a point where you will have to lose yourself to find yourself. That is when you must confront your deepest fear. Just as you have learnt to love yourself you must prepare to lose yourself. This is your ultimate act of sacrifice. You understand that your life does not belong to you. And this makes you love it even more. Now living your best possible life truly becomes your mission – and the only measurement of feeling true fulfilment.

You are now close, very close in fact, to fulfilment. You have already had glimpses of it – and you have started to feel its presence more and more poignantly. It is a mysterious, evasive feeling but one that is constant, and constantly making you blush. It permeates your life like a subtle perfume, like the light filling a room – like the presence of joy.

Your wonderful ability to be has now become a living example for others to see. By being you and fulfilling your mission you gift the world with your presence, and your life is the very proof of your fulfilment.

You inspire, you touch other lives and you share your wisdom and your joyful awareness with ease.

You live your life with the profound and blissful awareness of having achieved true fulfilment and the immense gratitude of having been able to do so.

* * * *

How does that feel? I hope you were able to get a glimpse of what it might mean to walk the journey to fulfilment. Often the transformation that takes place is difficult to put into words.

Suffice it to say that in this magical process you and your life will be completely transformed.

You enter a true partnership with life. You fall in love with your life and you become a co-creator of your life. That is the true meaning of being one with life. You live passionately – vibrantly. You express through your life and your life expresses through you.

To love being, to be in love with your life, is to step beyond being you into the miraculous field of living your life in service to Life – of giving your life as a gift back to Life. Everything you do at this level enriches you and enhances your life while affirming Life itself.

True fulfilment comes from being authentic and accomplishing your potential – thus fulfilling and honouring the unique opportunity that your life is.

(Explore more and get inspired with the wealth of insights and materials on the topic of being you, loving you and transcending you...that you will find at: www.BeingYouAndLovingYou.com)

LIVING A FULFILLING LIFE: IF NOT NOW, WHEN?

"Waking up is not a selfish pursuit of happiness, it is a revolutionary stance, from the inside out, for the benefit of all beings in existence."

– Noah Levine

We have explored together what it takes to embark on the journey to personal fulfilment.

We saw that it all starts with asking the right questions. We looked at what might happen when we fail to ask these questions. Then we had a glimpse at what to expect once we embark on this journey. I suppose the only question left is...Are you in?

You see... You either are or you aren't feeling fulfilled right now. And if you aren't, you are faced with a serious choice. True personal fulfilment involves presence and passion. You can't tell your life "I will live you tomorrow" or "I will love you tomorrow." You can't tell your mission, your purpose "I will be with you later." You have to be ready, open to it now. You have to commit to living your best possible life now.

The journey to fulfilment is not the easiest. It does require courage, honesty, a deep sense of wonder, the desire to overcome fears and the capacity to accept life's ephemeral and mysterious nature – and love it all the more for it.

To truly know fulfilment you must make the transition from living at the doing level to living at the Being level. Being successful has nothing to do with being fulfilled. Succeeding at Being has everything to do with it.

To truly succeed at Being you must go on a journey of self-discovery, and learn to celebrate your uniqueness, your richness, your unique expression, your feelings. You must learn to become a conscious co-creator of your life and then find the best ways to share your creation.

With this you move towards learning to love yourself and falling in love with your life. Once you learn to love yourself you must overcome your fear of losing yourself. This gives you the freedom to share yourself with the world.

By doing this you become an inspiration to others. You share the light of awareness with others. Finally you give back your life to Life with and for others – and in this you find ultimate fulfilment.

I don't know of a more wondrous journey – or one that is more worth it. You have been invited. The door has been opened for you. But only you can walk this journey and make your life the most extraordinary adventure of all. It is your life. Will you make it your fulfilment?

FINAL THOUGHT

If these pages have inspired you, you are probably ready to embark on the journey to fulfilment. Sometimes all we need is for someone to point the way. At other times we need someone to hold our hand as we learn how to fly on our own. I believe that Coaching can do that.

I believe that we live in a world where holding hands and learning from each other is soon becoming the norm. It is the only way in which we will be able to move forward. It is the only way in which we will learn, together, to truly Be. To be in love with our lives and to honour our potential. To find deep and lasting fulfilment. To share our richness and our beauty with everyone else, in joy. You can do it! See you there!

* * * *

Silvana is a successful Inspirational Coach, philosopher, writer and teacher.

More than anything else Silvana is a passionate human being driven by a deep commitment to create a better, happier world for everyone. She founded Life Coaching with Silvana to reach out and make her own contribution through empowering individuals to embrace and fulfil their potential, follow their dreams and live life with joy and gratitude. Silvana currently lives in the UK and divides her time between writing, coaching, group coaching, teaching, travelling, supporting humanitarian projects and conducting workshops and seminars.

To get in touch with Silvana, to know more about her Coaching practice, her projects and the events she organizes visit www.LifeCoachingWithSilvana.com

To get her book "Being You and Loving You – The Ultimate Guide To Fulfilment" together with free materials and more insights into the topic of fulfilment visit: www.LifeCoachingWithSilvana.com

Your Life Energy

AMAL INDI

I have 20 years of experience in the tech sector and corporate banking. In my previous life in the "Rat Race", I was waking up every day and going to a job that provided well for me. After some major changes in my life (including a divorce), I started recognizing that I wasn't intrinsically happy. I would be going about my day filled with negative thoughts and emotions. It felt as though they were taking over in a way, and I recognized how they were beginning to affect every moment of my day and every interaction with those around me. I refer to these as "Thought Bugs", which I will go on to explain later. These Thought Bugs were almost like a computer virus, affecting all the thoughts or, as one may say, programming in my mind. After recognizing these Bugs and studying them in myself for many years, I began to draw strong conclusions about how I could create positive change in my mind. This positive change in my thoughts would eventually lead to me leaving the "Rat Race" and starting on the mission of my life to share my new paradigm with those around me. I believe that we can change our minds and create a positive and uplifting life, not only for ourselves, but for those around us. I would love to share with you the basics of what I discovered, a new way of examining our thought patterns and how to drastically shift the energy around you (your Aura) so that you can lead a fantastic life!

GETTING STARTED ON YOUR OWN JOURNEY

When was the last time you really felt 100%? When I say 100%, I mean you wake up feeling a general positivity in your mood, you are looking forward to a new day, your interactions with people feel good, and you walk around feeling a general sense of purpose even with the simple tasks of getting groceries or whatever your work environment. You may think that you have no say in how you really feel. That deep down, you cannot control your thoughts and emotions. I know that this is not true. I developed a unique way of seeing our minds and how deeply they affect our energy. Have you heard of life energy, such as positive energy, negative energy, Aura energy, and universal energy? Read on!

WHAT MAKES US HUMAN?

Each one of us is a biological marvel of different cells, tissues, genes. These are the many working pieces that come together to create our human body. What really makes us human in a whole sense? We each possess an in-depth energetic landscape that we can't deny. This energetic pulse is used by scientists and technicians daily to perform tests and create pictures of our bodies and their functions. Think of the neuroscientists that connect our bodies to electrodes and measure our brain waves. That's part of it. We can't deny there is a part of us beyond just the tissues of our muscles and bones.

Did you know that surrounding you right now is an energy field that is all your own? This energetic field is referred to as your Aura. This Aura can be the beginning of a life that you love. Every human being has an energy field around them. We cannot see this field with the naked eye. However, we can see this field with an Aura machine. It's true! I personally have had mine captured and what was reflected back to me (in terms of energetic levels) was what I was truly feeling.

Your Aura and the energy you radiate is 100% in your control. Some days, you might feel positive and good, while other days, you may feel more negative and lower. These are your energy levels. They can vibrate high or low. It depends on you and your thoughts. Remember, with improvements to your mind and thoughts, your aura energy field will continuously change, thus altering the life you are leading.

YOUR AURA

Over the centuries of humans existing and contemplating our existence, many have acknowledged the fact that we have an energy that extends beyond our skin and flesh, which can actually interact with the world around us. This is referred to as your body's Aura. The Aura refers to the energy around your body that can be affected from the inside out or the outside in. When it is strong, the Aura around your body can extend quite a way beyond the barrier of your physical body (your skin). It can also manifest as different colours, depending on the emotional mood of the person. For example, when you are in a state of calm, then you will exude a white Aura. When you are in a state of anger, then you will exude a red Aura. Sometimes Auras may also be a combination of different colours. There is technology now that can show the colour and strength of someone's Aura. I have had mine checked. One day, it was light in colour and extended far beyond my body. This didn't surprise me as I feel I live in a state of calm, clear energy and my inner emotional landscape is positive. If you were to have an opportunity to get yours checked today what do you think the results would be? Strong and white? Or weak and maybe red? Maybe you feel like it may not show up at all.

This is what I want to teach you. This is my mission right now: To help you understand that you can empower yourself and create a strong, positive Aura that will not only affect your overall sense of well-being. It will affect your relationships, your business, and your life as a whole.

YOUR HUMAN SYSTEM

Through my own exploration, I began seeing and noticing a pattern in how my Aura was being affected by different things in my life. As I continued to study this in myself, it became clear to me that that there were specific things in play, and it was all rooted in my mind. Having a strong background in technology, I began to clearly see how our own minds behave like supercomputers. (Stay with me here!) Just like a super computer, we have our own operating system and the ability to run many programs at once. We are constantly juggling responsibilities, taking in the world around us, assessing how we feel, and determining what we need. The list could go on and on! Just take a moment right now: close your eyes and connect to all the "programs" open in your mind that are constantly running. Relate that to being connected to your own unique operating system of your mind. Now imagine that a computer virus was implanted into one of your programs and began affecting your thoughts. Computer viruses are designed to spread to all parts of a computer with the goal of eventually changing the computer, more often than not, making it completely dysfunctional. This is what can happen in your mind. A negative thought may enter your mind about something specific. Maybe a co-worker engages you in conversation about a rumour that someone is up for raise (one that you applied for) or on your coffee break the barista makes a mistake on your order and you feel it ruins your morning. I call these viruses of our thoughts Human Errors. In its most basic form, Human Errors can be outlined as the following emotions, or what I like to call Thought Bugs:

- Anger
- Suspicion
- Craving
- Comparison
- Low self-esteem
- Procrastination
- Getting stuck in negative thoughts

What it can be boiled down to is that these negative thought bugs can enter into your mind, which in turn creates negative energy. This leads to stress and a weakening of your Aura.

I'm sure you can think of a definitive moment, probably even within the last day or the last week, where you can see how your own errors were affecting your core system and negatively impacting the energy around you.

Luckily, we have a set of more positive emotions and various ways of reacting that counter the negative ones. I have identified these and aptly named them our Human Features.

Primary Human features that combat the errors include:

- Love and kindness
- Acceptance
- Forgiveness
- Courageousness
- Patience
- Authenticity
- Gratefulness

One can think of these features as a built-in tool box to combat negativity. This is always at our disposal! I want to help you identify where these positive emotions are in you, so that you may have access them and strengthen the energy that you are putting out into the world and your Aura.

Look, I am not a psychologist. I am not a therapist. I am, however, a believer in how we show up to our work and interact with those around us will have a deep impact on the life we are creating for ourselves. I have firsthand experience. I have taken myself from a place of negativity and darkness to a place of possibility. I have watched my newfound passions and work flourish, along with my relationships, personal and otherwise.

This is a different way of looking at things. This just isn't your usual "Be positive" message. This is connecting into the fact that as humans, we have a distinct design in place to help us truly create a good life for ourselves. The foundation of this is to truly feel happy and positive from the inside out, so that what we engage with is affected by our positive energy. Think of the last time you had an encounter with someone who you felt emitted a positive or happy energy? How did it make you feel? How did you react? You truly have the power to combat these negative thought processes (bugs) already in you! Don't you want to be the one truly living in your potential and sharing your positivity with everyone and everything in your life?

THE "AWESOME LIFE" IS WAITING FOR YOU!

Let's get down to business. Thanks for sticking with me. If you have continued reading to this point, then I want to applaud you! It means that you are deeply interested in living your best life.

Side effects of a mind free from negative Thought Bugs may include:

- General feelings of happiness and relaxation
- Genuine connections when meeting people
- A mind free from clutter
- A deep appreciation for the world and people around you
- High levels of productivity
- Willingness to learn new skills
- Gaining more contacts and connections with ease
- Feeling an authentic excitement for projects and self-development
- Being ready to rock your life!

These are just a few of the feelings available to you if you commit to removing negative Thought Bugs from your life, thus strengthening your energy and Aura from the inside out. I wouldn't be here today if I didn't do the work and experience the benefits of being on the other side of the process.

BRING LIGHT TO YOU

My hope for you is to learn how to identify your negative Thought Bugs and stop their process of multiplication. For you to empower yourself with positivity and strengthen your aura. For you to leave feelings of depletion behind and bring your energy back to 100%. For you to share your positive energy with the world and make it a better place!

Never forget: An Awesome Life is within your reach at all times. I believe it. In fact, I will go so far as to say I know it is. I have taken my own life and made it awesome by taking all I have outlined in my work and applying it to myself. Now it is your turn to turn up the positivity in your life and let your Aura shine!

I encourage you to check out my website, www.happinessmountain.com, to receive a free guide on removing your negative energy. In this guide, you will also be given a sneak peek into the app I am developing. The Happiness Mountain™ app will quickly become your new best friend! I developed the Happiness Mountain™ app to be a way to actually track those negative Thought Bugs and coach you to clear your worries and boost your energy levels! By giving you this important tool at your fingertips, I know you will be able to strengthen your energy and basically start living a more happy life! If you haven't guessed already, I love technology and its possibilities for enhancing our lives. I can't wait for you to be one of the first people to try this app and reap its benefits right away at www.happinessmountain.com/app.

BRINGING LIGHT TO YOU SO THAT YOU MAY BRING LIGHT TO THE WORLD

Now that I have given you some insight on how you can truly change your life by changing your own energy, I want to share the ways that Happiness Mountain™ can help you begin to apply these concepts. The process of understanding, application, and execution is key when committing to changing the way your mind functions and, over time, changing your aura.

Now that you know you have the power to change your life via your thoughts, I wonder why you wouldn't want to act now to change your life. Your own personal idea of an awesome life is within reach! I left behind an old way of living and being in order to start on a new path. I am confident that you have the power to do that for yourself as well. We all just need a little help. To be honest, I wish I had connected with these deeper levels of understanding regarding my thoughts and how they affect my life earlier. However, as we all know, timing is everything, especially when it comes to your advancement on both a personal level and a business one. Take this as a sign that it may be time for you to dive into these deep changes. The techniques, once you really begin to understand them, are quite straightforward. I know that you live a busy life and are striving to do your best. However, it takes commitment to change. Why not start now?

Happiness Mountain™ can offer you many tools to get started and help you dive deeper. The first step is easy! I encourage you to head over to my website www.happinessmountain.com to sign up and stay connected to the developments in my work. You will automatically receive an easy to follow guide on how to remove your negative energy, which will be delivered right to your inbox! You will also be given an automatic sneak peek into my app.

THE HAPPINESS MOUNTAIN™ APP

I am constantly inspired by how we connect online through different platforms and technologies. I believe that this can be the start to a great change in how we grow and develop. I designed the app as a convenient way for you to connect to your energy boosting practices on the go. We all spend some time on our phones scrolling and engaging on different platforms. Why not invest that time mindfully instead of mindlessly? The Happiness Mountain™ app, www.happinessmountain.com/app, helps you do that by having the tools you can utilize to boost your own positive energy available at any time!

Features include the following:

- Troubleshooting what is worrying you and replacing that worry with positivity

- Ways to resolve disputes without creating negative energy and affecting your Aura

- Aura boosting activities you can do on daily basis, while tracking your progress with your own private point system

- An emergency toolkit for handling sudden negative situations

- An easy guide to all the Thought Bugs and how to handle them available at a touch of your screen, so that you may continue to learn how you can change your thoughts to more positive ones and keep your positive energy high!

HAPPINESS MOUNTAIN™ FOR KIDS

Calling all parents and anyone who takes care of children! This work isn't just applicable to more mature minds and bodies. It can start when we are young! I am in the process of finishing development on a series of books for children that will cover all the core concepts of my work and Happiness Mountain™, so that we may share these valuable tools and concepts even with the developing minds of the next generation. Of course, there will be interactive games for children as well, because as we all know that some of the best learning happens when we are having fun! This goes for adults too, don't you think? Stay in the loop by connecting with me at www.happinessmountain.com.

MY NEXT BOOK

I am ready to dive deeper and share with you even more in my new book, *Happiness Mountain™: Double Your Happiness, Awesomeness and Spirituality*. In the book we are going to explore deeper than ever before. *Happiness Mountain™* will go more in depth on how you can harness the three levels of energy (Positive/Negative, Aura and Universal) to change your perspective and unlock your perfect life. I want to share with you the techniques and deep processes that will affect all aspects of your life. Remember those 'Negative Thought Bugs' I was talking about earlier? In my new book I will teach you not only how to eliminate them, I want to teach you how to protect yourself from future encounters with 'Negative Thought Bugs' therefore truly creating change in your life for the better. You will also learn techniques on how to recharge your energy, boost your aura and use your new skills for resolving conflicts and affecting your business.

I want you to harness the power of your personal Positive & Aura energies, learn to dance with the Universal energy that is always at your disposable and be able to live at a level of existence that falls in line with your ideal, perfect life. Take a look at the *Happiness Mountain™* diagram on the next page. You can define your perfect life as living with a high level of inner peace, the level of inner happiness. Your Awesome Life and Spiritual Life revolves around being of service to others and helping others. You can live a combination of all levels of the *Happiness Mountain™*. Whatever you personally define as perfection is where you have the power.

Happiness Mountain™ created by Amal Indi

Some might argue you cannot have a perfect life. I say you already have a perfect life and it is blocked by negative energy from coming into full fruition. This negative energy can be existing as a low self-esteem bug or a comparison bug. You may define perfect life as comparing to others. You may try to achieve things with craving energy. Please remember: You are already whole, complete and perfect. You cannot access your full power because of the negative energy being generated by your thoughts. When you learn to remove those negative thoughts as I teach you in *Happiness Mountain™*, you will realize how much power you have in life. This will be your turning point to harness the energy to power-up your personal, business and spiritual life! In the book I will give you all the tools and techniques to accomplish that. After reading my new book *Happiness Mountain™* you will be able to shift your life to a new paradigm that is not only accessible but exciting. How do you think it will feel to lead a perfect life? Can you think of even one thing that may change for the better if you decided to investigate how you could crush your negative energies, enhance your positive energies and essentially eliminate future worries from your life? ... Wow! I am excited for you just thinking about it myself! I know the profound changes it created for me in my life and I look forward to hearing how it affects yours.

YOU CAN LEAD AN AWESOME LIFE

My hope for you is to learn how to identify your negative Thought Bugs and stop their process of multiplication. For you to empower yourself with positivity and strengthen your aura. For you to leave feelings of depletion behind and bring your energy back to 100%. For you to share your positive energy with the world and make it a better place!

Never forget: The Awesome Life is within your reach at all times. I believe it. In fact, I will go as so far to say I know it is. I have taken my own life and made it perfect in my eyes by taking all I have outlined in my work and applying it to myself. Again, your negative thoughts may say your life is not perfect, which might include your low self-esteem, cravings, or comparison bugs blocking you. Don't let these bugs create negative energy. Instead, clear them and power-up the personal, business, or spiritual aspects of your life. Never forget you have the power over your own mind- NOT your negative Thought Bugs. Now it is time to power-up the positivity in your life and let your Aura shine!

I encourage you to check out my website, www.happinessmountain.com, for the opportunity to stay connected to the global community of people who have already begun to use this work to boost their positivity and create their

195

Awesome Life in their personal, business, and spiritual domains. I can't wait for you to begin using The Happiness Mountain™ App to start training your energy to stay positive and even get stronger. Of course, I encourage you to visit www.happinessmountain.com to stay connected and be in the know as to what is coming down the pipeline with this life changing work.

I have dedicated my life to bringing these concepts and work to you. I know you can change your energy and begin to not only affect your own life, but the entire world. I believe deeply that when as many people as possible align their energy to a higher, more positive state, then we can truly make a collective difference. Let's start today!

Amal Indi lives in Vancouver, Canada, and is the founder and CEO of Happiness Mountain™ Inc. After 20 years of working in technology and corporate banking, Amal is on a mission to give people the possibility to live with their full potential in their personal, business, and spiritual domains. He has found innovative techniques and tools to remove negative energy and power up your personal life, business life, and spiritual life. Ultimately, you can make the world a more awesome place for everyone. He believes that technology has the potential to transform the minds and energy of people and facilitate change. Amal wants to help people around the globe live a positive and enriching life through the energy-based tools and techniques of this innovative system he has developed to strengthen your energy and help you live a life full of happiness and potential. Find his story and work at www.happinessmountain.com.